Love to
Machine Appliqué

A Medley of Techniques

Caroline Price

Love to Machine Appliqué

A Medley of Techniques

By Caroline Price

American Quilter's Society
PO Box 3290
Paducah, Kentucky 42002-3290

Located in Paducah, Kentucky, the American Quilter's Society (AQS) is dedicated to promoting the accomplishments of today's quilters. Through its publications and events, AQS strives to honor today's quiltmakers and their work and to inspire future creativity and innovation in quiltmaking.

Editors: Karen Fail and Megan Fisher
Design, layout and illustrations: Susan Cadzow of Red Pepper Graphics
Photography: Andy Payne of Photographix, Sandy de Beyer
Cover Design: Michael Buckingham
Cover Quilt: **Delightful Dahlias** – by Caroline Price

Library of Congress Cataloging-in-Publication Data

Price, Caroline, 1948-
  Love to machine appliqué: a medley of techniques / by Caroline Price.
      p. cm.
  Summary: "A comprehensive quilting handbook on the tools needed, suitable stitches to use, and the best way to prepare fabric shapes. Includes nine original projects. Explains special procedures including bias strips, 3-D appliqué and reverse appliqué" -- Provided by publisher.
  ISBN 978-1-57432-956-8
  1. Machine appliqué. 2. Quilting--Patterns. I. Title.

TT779.P72 2008
746.46'041--dc22

                    2007050620

Additional copies of this book may be ordered from the American Quilter's Society,
PO Box 3290, Paducah, KY 42002-3290, or online at: www.AmericanQuilter.com.

Produced by:
QuiltWorks
Promoting Australian and New Zealand quiltmaking and quiltmakers
17 Peter Close, Hornsby Heights, NSW AUSTRALIA 2077

Printed in Hong Kong

Introduction

My first quilt was made many years ago, before I had learned anything about accurate seam allowances and templates. Even though the points didn't match, there was no quilting and I used a bagged method to back my quilt, I though it was just lovely. When I attended my first class, I was taught how to make a traditional sampler quilt by a lady I employed in my fabric store. Within an hour I was hooked. I couldn't wait to get home to try to interpret the hand appliqué blocks on my machine.

I live in an isolated area, approximately 70 kilometres from the nearest general store but, more importantly, a long way from a quilting shop. My husband John and I live in a rural sheep growing area that is quiet and very beautiful, with the soft colors of the Australian landscape around us. People imagine that our home would be decorated in a country style, but in fact, it is Asian influenced with lots of artefacts and paintings. Our daughter Valissa lived in Indonesia for quite a few years and after many visits, I fell in love with that country. I have also travelled extensively to the top and center of Australia, where the colors are much brighter and clearer than those of my local area. The brightness of the tropics has certainly influenced my quilting and I am drawn to clear, strong colors rather than the softer colors of my surroundings.

Because of my dread of hand sewing, everything that I learned I have adapted for the sewing machine. And when I go to major quilt shows, be they in Australia or overseas, I am always attracted to those quilts that incorporate appliqué. I have a great respect for hand appliqué but I don't have the time or patience to follow through. While I respect hand appliquérs and their skills, I remain in awe of beautifully made, machine appliquéd quilts.

The quilts in this book have been designed for those beginning to machine appliqué. Some quilts take a little more time and effort than others, but I have kept the shapes simple so that the skills can be learned without the problems associated with difficult motifs. Once the basic skills are acquired, you are free to break the rules and make the quilt of your dreams. When I am teaching, I always encourage students to interpret my quilts to reflect their own personality and then go ahead and fly and follow their own instincts. So I encourage you to fly and follow your dreams. Make quilts that reflect your surroundings but, most of all, have lots of fun.

Caroline Price

Love to Machine

CONTENTS

Appliqué

by Caroline Price

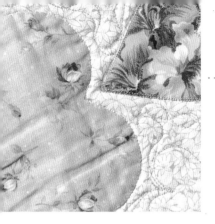

CHAPTER 1

Getting it all together
– basic supplies for machine appliqué

Now that you have decided to venture into the wonderful world of machine appliqué, it is time to collect the tools and equipment required to ensure the best possible results. Whether you plan to make a sensational, finely appliquéd heirloom quilt for your family, or want to have fun with a primitive blanket stitched project, read this chapter carefully, noting the equipment that you'll need. No doubt you'll have many of the supplies required, but some are likely to be new to you. Take time to practise with these new items before beginning any major project.

Sewing Machine

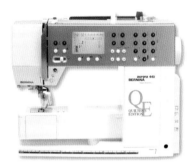

The quilts in this book were all sewn on a Bernina Aurora 440QE. I love my machine and we have a great relationship! I look after it faithfully by cleaning it, having it serviced regularly, changing needles often and using good quality threads. In turn, it repays me with hours of trouble free sewing. I often say that the only part of my house that I can guarantee is always clean is my machine!

For the machine appliqué stitches in this book, I used satin stitch (a basic zigzag stitch with reduced stitch length), blanket stitch, an adjustable blind hem stitch and straight stitch. Make sure your machine can do these stitches. I have also used fancy stitches such as grass stitch, but this and other decorative stitches are not as important as the basic ones. And remember too that it is important that your machine will sew an accurate ¼in seam allowance.

Presser Feet

You will need:

- **an open-toed embroidery or appliqué foot** that allows for good visibility when sewing appliqué stitches. This foot has a long, wide groove underneath, allowing bulkier stitches, such as satin stitch, to pass under the foot readily. On some machines, this foot is clear plastic.

- **a darning foot or quilting foot,** which is essential for free motion quilting. This foot is also used for free motion embroidery. With this foot and the feed dogs down, you can stitch in any direction without twisting the work around. Some older machines may not allow for the feed dogs to be lowered. Make sure you can cover them with a small plate. This plate does reduce the allowance underneath the needle, however. As an alternative, tape an old credit card over the feed dogs with a small hole cut out to allow the needle to pass through, thus maximising the allowance underneath the needle.

- **a walking foot or dual-feed foot** used for machine quilting. The walking foot helps feed the three layers of a quilt evenly through the machine. I always think of it as having feed dogs on the top of the work as well as underneath. A walking foot can also be used when stitching the binding in place.

- **a ¼in presser foot** is necessary for accurate piecing.

Needles and Pins

Choosing the right needle for the thread used is essential. Have a comprehensive selection of needles and experiment. Remember, the higher the number of the needle, the coarser it is. Change your needle often – eight hours is the recommended life span of any needle.

- For blind hem stitching with fine invisible thread, use a 60/8 needle.
- For piecing, try a 70/10 or 80/12 jeans needle. They have a sharp point and pierce the work cleanly.

- For appliqué and machine embroidery, try a rayon or polyester embroidery thread with an 80/12 jeans needle or a topstitch 80/12 needle.
- For heavier threads, such as jeans, topstitch or 30 weight rayon threads, try a topstitch 90/14 needle. Topstitch needles have a larger eye and groove that allow the thread to pass smoothly through them.
- For even thicker threads, such as Madeira Black Jewel, use a 100/16 needle.
- For metallic threads, use a Metafil or Heavy Metal needle. They have been treated to withstand the heat caused by the friction of the metallic thread.
- For pins, I like to use fine, sharp flower head pins. Because the flower head lies flat against the fabric, a ruler can be used with the pins in place.

Threads

I love threads! I am like a child in a candy shop when it comes to threads. I just can't resist them. You will find that the price of thread generally reflects the quality. Do use good quality threads, as they look and perform better. Keep in mind that the higher the number, the finer the thread.

Rayon threads

These are my favorite threads for satin stitch, as they are soft and 'spread a little', filling the stitching line. They also have a beautiful sheen. I use Madeira, Robinson Anton or Sulky. They come in different weights, with the most common being 30 or 40 weight. Refer to the Needles and Pins section for help when choosing a needle. Using the wrong needle can cause shredding.

Polyester threads

I have only recently discovered these wonderful threads (my addiction increases!). They also have a lovely sheen, like rayon threads, but don't break or 'shred' as often, as the polyester is stronger. I am currently experimenting with trilobal polyester threads by Superior Threads.

Cotton threads

Cotton threads are not just for piecing – they are also fabulous for machine appliqué. Cotton threads 'melt' into the quilt top much more successfully than polyester or rayon threads. There are some gorgeous variegated colors as well as plain. I use cotton threads by Superior Threads, Signature and YLI.

Monofilament

I find some students have a real love/hate relationship with these threads. Often the problem is wrong choice of needle or the machine top tension requires adjustment. Try using a 60/8 needle and loosening the top tension.

Monfilament is a very fine (.004) thread that comes in either nylon (such as Madeira Monofil or YLI Wonder) or polyester (MonoPoly by Superior Threads). I use monofilament thread for blind hem stitch and it is often my choice for ditch stitching when quilting. All of the threads come in clear or smoke colors. Use the clear for light color fabrics and smoke for dark colors. MonoPoly is more heat resistant than the nylon monofilament threads.

Bobbin threads

The thread that is used in the bobbin is just as important as the thread that shows on the top of the quilt. I use Madeira Bobbinfil and YLI Sew Bob. Recently, I've also worked with The Bottom Line by Superior Threads. This is a 60wt thread that comes in a wonderful array of colors, making it easy to match the top thread. Because Bottom Line threads are so fine, a lot more thread can be wound onto the bobbin. It is also a more compatible weight when using monofilament thread in the top of the machine.

When doing satin stitch or intense free machine embroidery, use rayon or polyester embroidery threads in the top of the machine and a suitable bobbin thread in the bobbin to prevent 'bulking'.

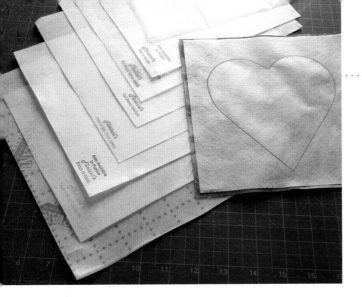

Stabilizers

There is a wealth of new stabilizers designed to prevent puckering and ensure that your work lies flat when you are doing any sort of intense stitching – especially satin stitch. The stabilizer is placed behind the work and removed after stitching. The stabilizer you choose depends on the choice of fabric, the type of stitching to be done and how the finished article is to be used. Whatever you are working on, remember the denser the stitch count, the stronger the stabilizer needs to be.

Tear away stabilizers are available in both iron-on and non-iron varieties. If you are using an iron-on stabilizer, be careful not to have your iron on too high a setting, as the stabilizer can become 'welded' in place, making its removal difficult. Start with an iron-on tear away stabilizer in your basic supplies.

Water-soluble stabilizers are really useful when doing intense stitching that would make a tear-away stabilizer difficult to remove. I use Vilene 541, sometimes called Wash-away, but there are many brands on the market. They are best used in conjunction with an embroidery hoop and can be simply rinsed away when the work is completed. When using water-soluble stabilizers, check what temperature the water should be when rinsing the stabilizer away. Include some in your basic supplies.

Freezer paper can also be used as a stabilizer. It irons on to the back of the background fabric, giving a firm base on which to work, and tears away easily. I use freezer paper for templates when sewing edges down with blind hem stitch. The shiny side sticks to fabric when applied with a medium, dry heat and you can trace directly on to the dull side. If the patterns need to be reversed, you can also draw on the shiny side with a pencil such as a Staedtler Omnichrom or any pencil that is designed to be used on a plastic surface.

To cut out several of the same appliqué shape at once, draw or trace the shape on freezer paper first. Then cut several pieces of freezer paper slightly larger than the shape. Staple these together with the drawn pattern and cut several layers of paper at the same time.

Double-sided Fusible Web

For satin or buttonhole stitch, keep appliqué shapes in place on the background fabric and prevent fraying with fusible web. There are quite a few brands of fusible web available. In the United States, Wonder Under and Heat n Bond are readily available. The most commonly used in Australia and New Zealand is Vliesofix.

Keep fusible web in a sealed zip locked bag to prevent the layer of glue separating from the paper backing. This is especially important in humid climates. I buy my fusible web in rolls only 12in (30cm) wide rather than any wider, just so that I can seal it in this manner.

Template Plastic

If the appliqué shapes are going to be used several times, it is best to to trace each shape from the original appliqué pattern on to clear template plastic to make a hard template for each shape. It is much easier to trace an appliqué shape on to either fusible web or freezer paper using a template rather than trace each appliqué motif separately from the original pattern.

To hold templates in place, especially when tracing small shapes, try using tiny dabs of a putty-like pressure sensitive adhesive, such as Blu Tack or Fun Tack.

After cutting templates, use the edge of your scissors, fine sandpaper or a nail file to make sure the edges are smooth and accurate.

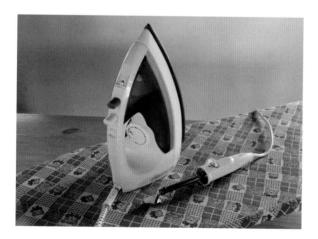

Irons

An iron with a sharp point is an invaluable tool when machine appliquéing. Choose one with both steam and dry features. My absolute favorite for tiny pieces and bias strips is the Clover mini-iron, as it has saved me many burnt fingers!

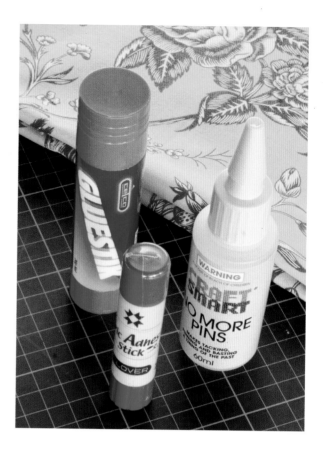

Glues and Starch

Glue sticks are used when preparing shapes for appliqué with freezer paper. Choose a glue stick that is marked as suitable for use with fabric. If in doubt, test it with scraps of fabric to see if it causes the color to run.

Spray starch acts as an extra stabilizer, helping to prevent distortion and keeping everything firm when machine appliquéing. Spraying fabric with starch before cutting bias strips also helps keep the strip edges crisp and I find that they go through my bias makers more readily. Spray starch is also helpful when piecing. Some fabrics have a much softer hand than others. Spraying them with starch allows you to piece them with firmer fabrics much more readily.

'No More Pins' by Craft Smart allows you to glue down bias strips lightly, without pinning them. Wait until

Tip: Test fabrics for colorfastness once the glue is applied and use a glue stick that is clearly marked for use with fabric.

the liquid is dry before stitching (a hair dryer is useful if you are in a hurry). The great benefit of this product is that it washes away completely without leaving a ridge that can result when craft glue is used. You can also re-position strips without having to worry about the glue residue, as it simply rinses away.

Marking Pens and Pencils

Marking pens and pencils are used to transfer patterns to the background fabric or mark quilting lines. There are so many on the market it can make you dizzy!

A retractable pencil can be used to mark placement guides for appliqué shapes. I normally draw these lines slightly inside the stitching line so they are covered once the shapes are appliquéd.

Clover makes a white pen for use on dark backgrounds that irons out and is very handy.

I use a blue water-erasable pen for marking quilting lines if required, but remember that if these lines are ironed before they are washed out, permanent, faint yellowish lines may result.

Bias Tape Makers

There are several tools on the market for making bias tape, which can be used for Celtic work, vines and stems.

Bias tape makers: a bias strip of fabric is inserted through the tape maker and pressed with an iron as it emerges. The edges of the strip are already folded when it emerges and pressing holds them in place. The tape is ready to be pinned or glued in place with a product such as No More Pins or double-sided fusible web tape.

Quilter's press bars (yellow and blue in the photo above): these come in either metal or heatproof nylon plastic in five sizes ranging from ⅛in (3mm) to ½in (12mm). Bias fabric strips are folded and stitched in half; then the press bar is inserted into the tube of fabric with the seam in the middle and pressed into bias tape.

There are so many gizmos on the market for machine appliqué that we should always remember the old adage 'buyer beware'. Try to buy small quantities of all of the basic supplies listed in this section and test them, both for yourself and your machine.

CHAPTER 2

Preparing shapes for machine appliqué

Before preparing shapes for appliqué, you need to decide what type of appliqué you want, as each type requires different preparation.

If you want to have your work resemble hand appliqué or you're planning to work straight edge appliqué, you will need to have shapes with a prepared edge. Here, the seam allowance is turned under on each shape before stitching. To prepare shapes in this manner, use one of the freezer paper methods or face the shape with a wash-away product. The goal is to get the edge as smooth as possible.

However, if you are planning to edge each shape with satin stitch, buttonhole stitch or another decorative stitch, then you only need to attach the raw-edged shape to the background with a fusible web, as the stitching seals the raw edges.

♥ Method 1: freezer paper method with glue

YOU WILL NEED:

- FREEZER PAPER
- RETRACTABLE PENCIL
- FABRIC AND PAPER SCISSORS
- CHINAGRAPH (OR SIMILAR) PENCIL (OPTIONAL)
- GLUE STICK SUITABLE FOR FABRIC
- TAILOR'S AWL OR SMALL BAMBOO STICK
- WATER SPRAY BOTTLE
- PRESSING CLOTH

Tip: With asymmetrical shapes, you will need to prevent creating a mirror image. Use a light box or tape the appliqué pattern to a window so that you can see the wrong side of the shape with the aid of light. Trace the pattern on to the other side of the paper. Then trace each shape on to the dull side of freezer paper.

Tip: To avoid double work with asymmetrical shapes, use a pencil that will write on glass or plastic, such as a Staedtler Omnichrom or a Chinagraph pencil and trace each shape on to the shiny side of the freezer paper.

1. Trace the template on to the dull side of the freezer paper. If a template is not being used, simply place the appliqué pattern underneath the freezer paper and trace around each shape. Cut out the freezer paper template carefully on the pencil line.

2. Using a dry iron, press the shiny side of the freezer paper shape to the wrong side of the chosen fabric. Cut the fabric shape out, adding a scant ¼in seam allowance. Snip the inner concave curves. Sometimes several small nicks are necessary to maintain a smooth curve when the fabric is turned over on to the freezer paper template.

4. Roll the fabric seam allowance over the edge of the freezer paper template, smoothing the edges as you go with your fingers. If an edge is to lie underneath another appliqué shape, there is no need to turn the seam allowance over. (See Chapter 3 for more information.) Using a tailor's awl or small bamboo stick, gather the outer convex curves. Tiny gathers will help maintain a smooth, crisp edge.

3. Run a glue stick lightly around the edge of the freezer paper template and the fabric seam allowance.

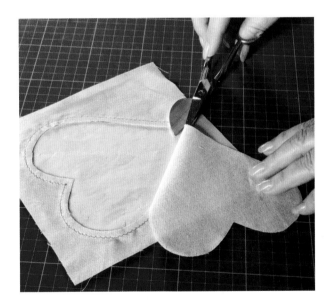

5. After appliquéing the shape in place on the background fabric with a blind hem stitch (see Chapter 4), cut away the background fabric leaving a ¼in seam allowance. Moisten the freezer paper with a spray of water to dissolve the glue. Leave for 10 minutes, then carefully remove the freezer paper.

♥ Method 2: freezer paper without glue

This technique is most suitable for appliqué shapes that don't have tiny, tight curves, as fingers can be burnt very easily!

YOU WILL NEED:

- FREEZER PAPER
- FABRIC AND PAPER SCISSORS
- RETRACTABLE PENCIL
- SMALL IRON E.G. CLOVER MINI-IRON
- PINS

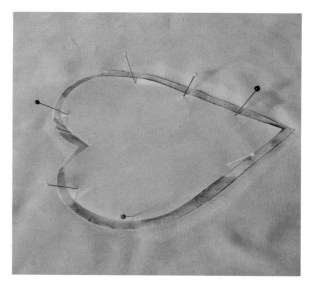

2. Place the freezer paper template on the wrong side of the fabric – this time with the shiny side up. Pin the paper and fabric in place on an ironing board. The pins should be slanted, piercing the freezer paper, fabric and ironing board cover to hold the layers firmly in place.

1. Trace around the template on the dull side of the freezer paper. If a template is not being used, simply place the appliqué pattern underneath the freezer paper and trace around each shape. Cut out the freezer paper template carefully on the pencil line. If the shape is symmetrical, lightly press the freezer paper template to the wrong side of the fabric. If the shape is asymmetrical, iron it to the right side of fabric to avoid creating mirror imaged shapes. Cut the fabric shape out adding a ¼in seam allowance. Peel the freezer paper template away from the fabric.

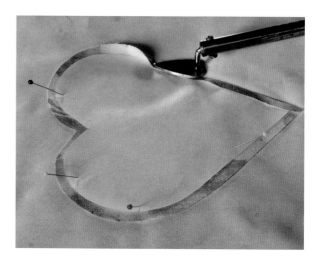

3. Use the side of the iron to press the seam allowance over on to the freezer paper to hold it in place. Let the fabric run ahead of the iron on curves, so that they turn over smoothly. Appliqué the shape in place, cut away the background fabric with a ¼in seam allowance and remove the freezer paper template. (See Step 5 in Method 1.)

Method 3: face the shape with water-soluble stabilizer

With this method, it is very easy to create appliqué shapes that have perfectly smooth edges.

YOU WILL NEED:
- WATER-SOLUBLE STABILIZER
- PEN OR PENCIL THAT WILL SHOW UP ON STABILIZER E.G WATER-ERASABLE PEN

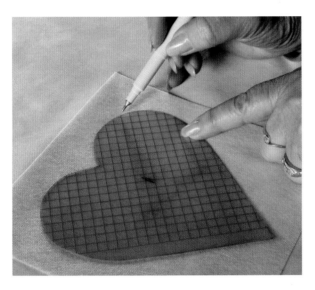

1. Trace around the template on a piece of water-soluble stabilizer with a water-erasable pen.

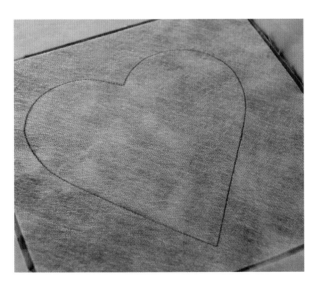

2. Pin the water-soluble stabilizer on top of the right side of the fabric. Stitch around the shape on the line using a small straight stitch and thread that closely matches the fabric.

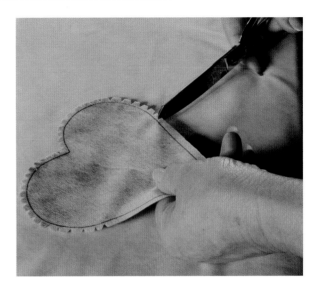

3. Cut out the shape, leaving a ¼in seam allowance. Make small nicks in the seam allowance on curves and any inverted points, taking care not to cut the stitching.

4. Cut a slit in the water-soluble stabilizer layer only and turn the shape right side out. If necessary, smooth out the edges with a knitting needle that has a large rounded end. The appliqué shape can then be stitched in place as required and the water-soluble stabilizer will dissolve when the quilt top is rinsed.

❤ Method 4: double-sided fusible web

Fusible web permanently sticks the appliqué shape to the background fabric and helps prevent fraying around its edges.

YOU WILL NEED:

- DOUBLE-SIDED FUSIBLE WEB
- PENCIL
- SCISSORS

1. Trace the appliqué shape on to the paper backing of lightweight fusible web. Remember that this shape will be mirror imaged when finally sewn in place. To avoid this, place the template wrong side up on the paper backing or trace a mirror image of the original design. (See the Tip on page 12.) Cut out the shape, leaving a seam allowance of approximately ¼in around it. **Do not cut on the line.**

> Tip: To prevent the appliqué shape fraying when removing the paper backing, score the paper across its center with a pin. The paper will now peel away easily.

2. Press the shape to the wrong side of the chosen fabric following the manufacturer's instructions. When cool, cut out the shape carefully on the drawn line.

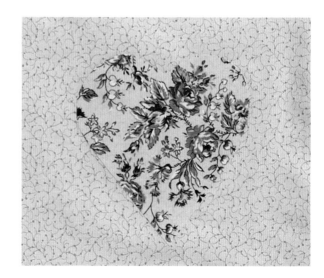

3. Peel off the backing paper, and place the shape in its correct position on the background fabric. Fuse it in place with an iron, ready for appliquéing. Take care not to touch the glue side of the double-sided fusible web with the iron, as it is very difficult to remove.

Love to Machine Appliqué

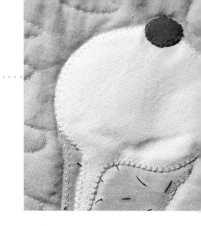

CHAPTER 3

Placing and layering appliqué shapes

After the appliqué shapes have been prepared, it's time to position and layer them accurately on the background fabric, ready for stitching in place.

When preparing shapes, don't forget that you shouldn't turn under the seam allowances that will be covered by other appliqué shapes.

Choose a background fabric suitable for your project. Many of the background fabrics in this book are dark and dramatic, providing a strong contrast with the appliqué. When the quilt calls for a softer contrast, choose a light colored hand dyed fabric or a soft tone-on-tone for the background. Of course, you are free to experiment and use any background fabric you wish, although it would be wise to stay away from vibrant, large print fabrics. Pre-wash and press your chosen background fabric to give the best surface for the appliqué.

Many quilters mark the appliqué pattern directly on the background fabric. This is not recommended for machine appliqué, as the lines may not be quite covered by the appliqué and you risk not being able to remove them after the work has been completed.

ORGANISE THE APPLIQUÉ SHAPES

1. Place the complete pattern on a firm ironing board. Place the background fabric over the pattern. If the pattern can be seen clearly through the fabric, fuse shapes directly on to the fabric. When using shapes with prepared edges, pin them in place on the background fabric with the pins placed perpendicular to the edge of the shape.

2. For layered appliqué – when the shapes overlap – the underneath shape is fused or pinned in place first. Shapes that are to be overlapped often have the extra seam allowance indicated with a dotted line on the pattern. This added allowance will tuck in neatly underneath the shape above it. Include the extra seam allowance when tracing the shapes on to fusible web or add it yourself if it is not provided.

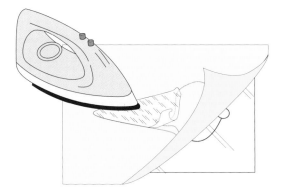

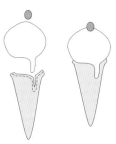

Shapes for the ice cream cone in Sun & Surf (page 63) traced on to fusible web, with the extra seam allowance indicated by the broken line

Tip: If you only have a section of a symmetrical pattern, draw a complete pattern for this step. For some projects in this book e.g. *Sun & Surf*, the placement of the appliqué shapes in the center of the quilt is not specified exactly, so a complete pattern isn't needed and each shape can be dealt with separately.

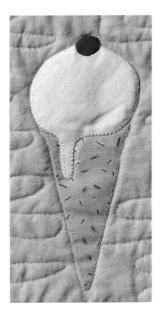

Finished ice cream cone with the extra seam allowance on the cone tucked under the ice cream.

3. On more complex patterns, a numbering system may be provided to indicate the stitching sequence. If it isn't provided, consider the order in which to place the shapes and create your own sequence. Consider also which shapes will overlap others and if they require extra seam allowances added.

4. If you can't see the pattern clearly through the background fabric or if the pattern is more complex, use an appliqué mat to 'build' the appliqué. When the appliqué motif is complete, simply peel away the appliqué mat and the motif is ready for use.

To use a mat, place the original pattern (not the mirror image used for preparation of fusible web) under the mat. Identify which shapes need to be on the bottom layer e.g shapes 2 and 4 for the umbrella (below left). Remove the paper from the back of the shapes and place them in position according to the pattern. Iron for a few seconds to allow them to fuse to the appliqué mat.

Choose the next layer of shapes, remove the paper and put them in place according to the pattern e.g shape 3 for the umbrella. Press the sections that are overlapping so they will fuse to the bottom layer. Continue in this manner until the entire appliqué motif is complete. When cool, you can remove it from the mat and it is ready to fuse into place on the background fabric.

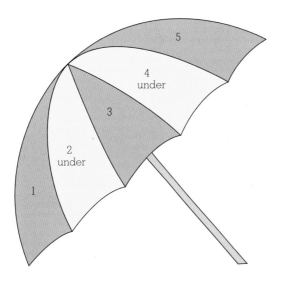

Pattern for the umbrella in Sun & Surf (page 63) with numbers indicating the sewing sequence. Shapes 2 and 4 go underneath the adjacent shapes and require seam allowances to be added.

Umbrella from Sun & Surf being 'built' on an appliqué mat.

Love to Machine Appliqué

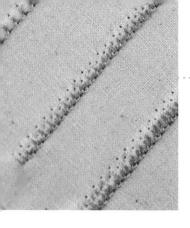

CHAPTER 4

Stitch samples

Many modern machines have a wonderful array of both functional and decorative stitches that you can use in machine appliqué projects. Add the huge variety of different threads available today and all you need for success is your own creativity.

Sample 1: blind hem stitch

The blind hem stitch is used in conjunction with prepared edge appliqué shapes (see Chapter 2) and bias strips (see Chapter 5). Use this stitch when you want your project to have the look of traditional appliqué.

Sample of blind hem stitch appliqué

MACHINE SET UP

- STITCH – BLIND HEM STITCH
- STITCH WIDTH – 1.0 (TINY)
- STITCH LENGTH – 0.5 – 1.0 (TINY)
- FOOT – OPEN-TOED APPLIQUÉ FOOT
- TOP THREAD – MONOFILAMENT
- BOBBIN THREAD – LIGHTWEIGHT BOBBIN OR POLYESTER THREAD
- NEEDLE - 70/10 JEANS NEEDLE OR SIZE 60/8 UNIVERSAL NEEDLE

START STITCHING

Start stitching on a straight edge of the appliqué. The left swing of the needle should just catch the appliqué shape with the small straight stitches positioned off the shape and running along its edge on the background fabric. It is important to catch both inner and outer points and corners. Mirror image the stitch if necessary so that the left swing of the needle catches the appliqué. To finish, stitch over the starting stitches to lock off the work.

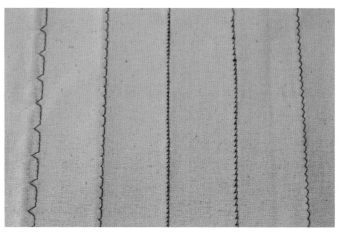

Samples of invisible appliqué stitches. (The monofilament thread has been replaced with a colored thread to make the stitching easier to see.) From the left: i) Blind hem stitch – default setting ii) Blind hem stitch – width 1.0, length 1.0, iii) Super stretch stitch – default setting iv) Super stretch stitch – width 1.0, length 4.0 v) Zigzag stitch – width 1.1, length 1.9

Tip: Using a cotton thread in the bobbin may present problems for some machines, as it is much heavier than monofilament thread and will keep showing on the surface of the work.

Tip: If your machine will not allow you to reduce the length and width of the blind hem stitch sufficiently for invisible appliqué, try using a super stretch stitch, or perhaps as a last resort, a very open (length) and narrow (width) zigzag stitch. Adjustments may need to be made to the indicated length and width of these stitches.

⬭ Sample 2: satin stitch

Sample of satin stitch appliqué

Satin stitch is used with raw edged shapes that have been backed with fusible web. Some of the newer computerised machines have a satin stitch programmed in; otherwise use a zigzag stitch and adjust the stitch length and width. Satin stitch always requires a stabilizer behind the work — **think satin stitch, think stabilizer.**

MACHINE SET UP

- STITCH – SATIN STITCH OR ZIGZAG STITCH
- STITCH WIDTH – START WITH 2.0MM
- STITCH LENGTH – AS FOR BUTTONHOLES
- FOOT – OPEN-TOED APPLIQUÉ FOOT
- TOP THREAD – RAYON OR COTTON MACHINE EMBROIDERY THREAD
- BOBBIN THREAD – LIGHTWEIGHT BOBBIN THREAD TO MATCH BACKGROUND FABRIC
- NEEDLE – TO SUIT TOP THREAD
- TOP TENSION – LOWER SLIGHTLY TO GIVE A ROUNDED STITCH
- BOBBIN TENSION – TIGHTEN, OR THREAD THROUGH THE 'FINGER' ON THE BOBBIN CASE

START STITCHING

1. Bring the bobbin thread to the top of the work. Stitch approximately 10 very small straight stitches. These small stitches lock off the work so the top and bottom threads can be trimmed away flush with the surface of the work**.** Alternatively, you can take both threads to the back of the work and tie off and trim later.

Tip: You can use locking stitches to secure the thread. Stitch just on the appliqué shape in the opposite direction that the satin stitch will begin, trim the threads, turn the work around and satin stitch. The satin stitch will then cover the straight, locking stitches. When one shape is completed, sew locking stitches on adjoining appliqué pieces without cutting the thread, even if the satin stitch is in a different colour.

Tip: Use lightweight bobbin thread in the bobbin where possible. It is fine, the bobbin will take a lot more thread and work does not 'bulk up' underneath as it may with a regular thread. Using specialized bobbin thread also means that you can change the top thread color without having to change the bobbin thread. However, your machine manual may recommend using the same thread in the bobbin as on top. Experiment to see what works best.

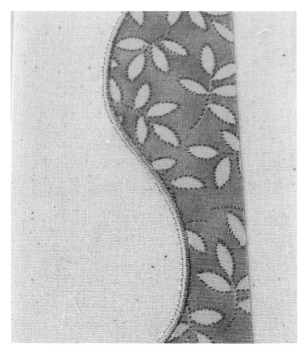

Satin stitch on curves

2. When satin stitching on curves, pivot the work to keep the stitches perpendicular to the edge of the appliqué shape. To pivot, stop with the needle on the background fabric in the wide part of the curve (i.e. the convex or outer curve), lift the presser foot, turn the work slightly and do a few more stitches. When pivoting on the inner (concave) curves, exactly the same procedure is followed but the needle is stopped when it is on the appliqué so that the pivoting occurs on the appliqué shape.

Satin stitch on tight curves

3. To stitch tight curves, sew until the needle is nearly to the middle of the curve. By manipulating the hand wheel, keep returning the needle to the same center point on the appliqué and pivoting on the outside edge to create a fan effect, as shown.

Satin stitch on pointed corners

4. For points, it is not necessary to taper the stitch. Satin stitch to the top of the point, pivoting when necessary. Leave the needle down and turn your work. The corner is now covered. Stop with the needle in the work and check the throw of the needle – make sure it is going to swing to the left – then continue sewing. If the needle is going to swing to the right, simply move the fabric so that the needle goes into the work at the correct point.

Direction of satin stitch with pointed corners.

Tip: For some stitches you will need to alter the tension on your machine for the best results. If the bobbin thread is showing, reduce the top tension and tighten the bobbin tension if necessary. (If the bobbin case has a 'finger', put the thread through the hole in it to automatically increase the bobbin tension.) For each stitch, do a test first and record what settings you used for different threads. Remember when adjusting tensions, **right is tight, left is loose.**

☰ Sample 3: blanket stitch

Blanket stitch appliqué. Note the small stitches used to turn the corner on the square.

Blanket stitch uses raw edged appliqué shapes backed with fusible web. This stitch is often used in projects for a more primitive or country look. If your machine doesn't have a blanket stitch, an altered zigzag stitch can be used to achieve a similar finish. Some machines require a lightweight tear away stabilizer behind the work.

MACHINE SET UP
- STITCH – BLANKET STITCH
- STITCH WIDTH – DEFAULT OR PERSONAL CHOICE
- STITCH LENGTH – DEFAULT OR PERSONAL CHOICE
- FOOT – OPEN-TOED APPLIQUÉ FOOT
- TOP THREAD – COTTON OR RAYON MACHINE EMBROIDERY THREAD
- BOBBIN THREAD – SAME AS TOP THREAD
- NEEDLE – DETERMINED BY THREAD

START STITCHING
1. To start and end blanket stitch, sew a tiny straight stitch or pull the threads to the back of the work and tie them off. I prefer not to use the locking stitch that some machines have, as it can create a visible knot of thread.
2. As you sew, keep the stitches perpendicular to the edge of the appliqué shape, making sure inner and outer points and corners are covered by a stitch.
3. Reduce the stitch width a little before reaching a corner point or tight curve and increase it again

once you are past it, to prevent the stitches crossing over each other.
4. Pivot when required, as detailed in the instructions for satin stitch.

> Tip: Use a blanket stitch that doesn't sew backward and forwards on itself, as this can cause problems when turning corners. Some machines will also need to have the blanket stitch mirror imaged.

☰ Sample 4: grass stitch

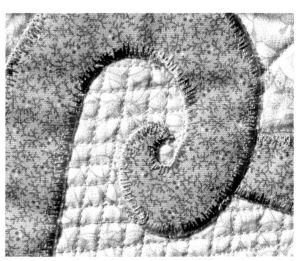

Sample of grass stitch appliqué

Grass stitch is a programmed stitch on many new machines. Different models produce different results. Like satin stitch, always use a stabilizer behind the work.

MACHINE SET UP

- STITCH – GRASS STITCH
- STITCH WIDTH – DEFAULT (REDUCE IF PREFERRED)
- STITCH LENGTH – DEFAULT (REDUCE IF PREFERRED)
- FOOT – OPEN-TOED APPLIQUÉ FOOT
- TOP THREAD – RAYON MACHINE EMBROIDERY THREAD
- BOBBIN THREAD – LIGHTWEIGHT BOBBIN THREAD
- NEEDLE – DETERMINED BY THREAD

START STITCHING

1. Sew with grass stitch. To pivot, follow the instructions for satin stitch.
2. If you don't have a programmed grass stitch on your machine, blanket stitch can be altered to give interesting effects.

On some machines, you can program the stitches into the memory, i.e. one stitch + one wider stitch, to avoid having to sew around the shape twice.

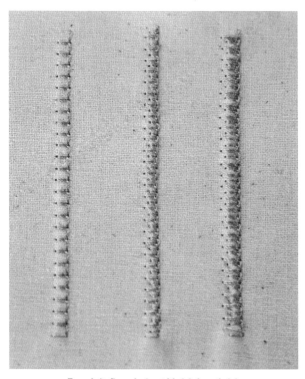

From left: Sample 1: width 3.0, length 3.0.
Sample 2 : width 3.0, length 3.0. Second run: width 2.0, length 3.0
Sample 3: width 3.0, length 3.0. Second run: width 4.0, length 3.0

◉ Sample 5:
free motion stitching

Sample of free motion stitching. The center of the heart has three lines of straight free motion stitching. On the outside edge of the heart is 'sketchy' free motion stitching. The left side shows the first run of stitching with a dark thread. The right side shows the second run with a dark thread filling in the gaps. A lighter thread was used for the third run around the top right curve.

Free motion stitching uses raw edged appliqué shapes backed with fusible web. Back the work with a firm stabilizer to prevent it from puckering. Iron-on stabilizer and freezer paper are good weights but unfortunately can't be removed from behind the intense stitching. Net (not tulle, as it is too soft) is a good option and firm water-soluble stabilizer is another. Use a double layer of water-soluble stabilizer if necessary. Net can be trimmed away from around the intense stitching at the back of the finished work and a firm water-soluble stabilizer can be rinsed away.

MACHINE SET UP

- STITCH – STRAIGHT STITCH
- STITCH LENGTH – NOT SET
- FOOT – QUILTING OR DARNING FOOT
- TOP THREAD – COTTON OR RAYON MACHINE EMBROIDERY THREAD
- BOBBIN THREAD – LIGHTWEIGHT BOBBIN THREAD
- NEEDLE - DETERMINED BY THREAD
- LOWER OR COVER FEED DOGS
- ADJUST THE FOOT TENSION IF POSSIBLE TO ITS LOWEST POINT IF RECOMMENDED IN THE MANUAL FOR YOUR SEWING MACHINE

1. To start and stop stitching when sewing free motion, bring the bobbin thread to the top and stitch 8 – 10 tiny stitches. These tiny stitches will lock the work. Both the top and bobbin threads can then be trimmed even with the surface.

2. Maintain an even, moderate to fast speed. I find it difficult to sew with a slow speed when doing free motion – both the length of stitches and line of sewing become erratic. Look a little ahead of the presser foot rather than at the needle itself.

3. To hold an appliqué shape in place, sew a free motion straight stitch close to the edge of the appliqué and then go over it again. This second, or even third, line of stitching has the advantage of catching the appliqué shape if the first row was a little 'off line'. A third line of stitching gives the line even greater definition.

4. For a sketchy, filled in look when stitching around curves, lightly draw the direction of the stitching on the appliqué with a pencil. The first 'run' of stitching will cover the pencil lines. A second 'run' of stitching provides the opportunity to fill in gaps and even out the coverage. I like to do a third 'run' of stitching with a different shade of thread to give a more dimensional look.

⊖ Sample 6: twin needling

Twin needling is used with raw edged appliqué shapes backed with fusible web. Use iron-on interfacing as the stabilizer behind the work to prevent puckering, as it is too difficult to remove tear away interfacing from behind twin needling without distorting the stitches. Alternatively, a water-soluble stabilizer can be used if preferred.

MACHINE SET UP

- STITCH – DECORATIVE STITCH E.G. FEATHER
- STITCH LENGTH – PERSONAL CHOICE
- FOOT – OPEN-TOED APPLIQUÉ FOOT
- TOP THREAD – TWO REELS OF THE SAME THREAD SPOOLING IN DIFFERENT DIRECTIONS
- BOBBIN THREAD – ONE OF THE TOP THREADS
- NEEDLE – 1.6MM OR 2.0 MM TWIN NEEDLE, SIZE 80

PREPARATION

Make sure that the stitch you select (e.g. feather stitch) will not be too wide for the hole plate of your machine when doing twin needling. Check the

Sample of twin needling appliqué

indicator on your machine or slowly turn the hand wheel to lower the needle and check the width of the stitch to make sure the twin needle has space to fit into the hole plate.

START STITCHING

1. Align the edge of the appliqué shape with the center of the appliqué foot so that the decorative stitch will sew evenly on either side of the edge.

2. Pivot slowly around corners and curves. Pivoting is done with the needles just out of the work and carefully moving the appliqué shape. Stitches such as a feather stitch are pivoted when the outer swing is on the outer side of the curve. For inner curves, pivot when the inner swing is on the inner side of the curve.

3. Pull all threads to the back of the work and tie off.

Tip: The secret to twin needling is to keep the threads as separate as possible. Place the left thread through the left side of the tension disc and the right thread through the right side (depending on your machine). One thread will go through the thread keeper just above the needle and the other bypasses it. The twin needle can then be threaded.

CHAPTER 5

Special techniques

Often appliqué patterns include narrow stems and vines or shapes that are outlined with bias tape, such as in stained glass techniques. There are many helpful tools available to assist in making perfect bias tape suitable for Celtic work, vines and stems. Try several methods and see which one works best for you.

♡ Technique 1: bias tape appliqué

Fusible web permanently sticks the shape to the background fabric and helps prevent fraying around its edges.

Sample of hearts applied with bias tape and blind-hem stitch

YOU WILL NEED:

- BIAS TAPE MAKER, QUILTER'S PRESS BARS OR THIN CARDBOARD
- OPEN-TOED APPLIQUÉ FOOT
- IRON WITH POINTED TIP OR MINI-IRON
- DOUBLE- SIDED FUSIBLE WEB TAPE
- 'NO MORE PINS'
- SPRAY STARCH
- RULER WITH 45 DEGREE LINE
- NEEDLE DETERMINED BY THREAD
- THREAD TO SUIT STYLE OF STITCHING

PREPARATION

1. Remove the selvages from the fabric. To cut bias strips of fabric, align the 45 degree line on a ruler with the edge of the fabric. Make the first cut and discard the first triangle of fabric. Move the ruler along, cutting strips at the desired width.

2. Join the bias strips at 45 degrees with two close lines of stitching. Trim the seam allowance.

3. Insert the bias strip into the bias maker along with the paper backed fusible web strip. As the fabric strip and fusible strip come out of the bias maker, the edges of the fabric strip are turned under and the fusible web is ironed on at the same time, creating bias tape that is ready to use. Remove the paper to position the tape around the shape to be appliquéd.

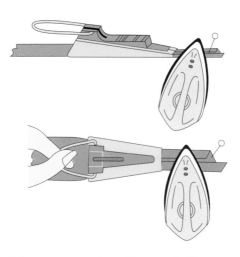

Using a bias tape maker and iron to make bias tape. The tape emerges with the fusible web tape included.

4. Quilter's press bars can also be used to create bias tape. Cut the bias strips of fabric twice the width of the bar being used plus ⅝in. Fold the strip in half, wrong sides together and sew the long edges together with a ¼in seam. Press the seam allowance open and trim back to ⅛in. Insert the press bar into the center of the tube with the seam allowance rolled to the center of the back of the bar. Iron the tube of fabric with the press bar inside and continue to pull the fabric over the tube, ironing as the fabric moves along. Add thin strips of fusible web or a thin line of 'No More Pins' to the wrong side of the bias tape just before you are ready to use it.

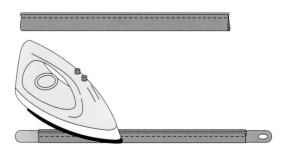
Creating bias tape with bias bars

5. If you don't have either a bias tape maker or quilter's press bars or you need to make bias tape wider than these tools allow, then thin, firm cardboard can be cut to the desired finished width. Cut the bias strips of fabric ½in wider than the cardboard, allowing for a ¼in seam allowance on both sides. Lightly spray the bias strip of fabric with starch, then center the cardboard strip on its wrong side. Press the seam allowances over the edges of the cardboard until they are dry. Keep moving the cardboard strip along the length of the bias fabric strip until all edges are turned over. Make extra cardboard strips as

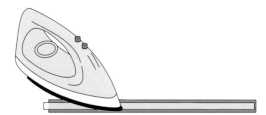
Creating bias tape with a cardboard strip

required, as the spray starch softens their edges. Add strips of double-sided fusible web to the wrong side of the bias tape just before you are ready to use it.

START STITCHING

1. If you have not added strips of fusible web to the bias tape, run a thin line of 'No More Pins' along the drawn pencil line on the work where the bias tape will be placed. With stained glass work, the line of glue will be on the edge of the appliqué shapes.

2. Carefully place the bias tape on the background fabric and iron or glue it in place. Now pin the tape in place – it can move ahead of the presser foot if not secured properly. For curves, gently stretch the edge, easing it to fit the curve. Miter any corners.

3. Where possible, tuck the beginning and end of the bias strip under another appliqué shape. Otherwise, leave a little tail of bias tape at the start. With a heart, for example, gently ease the bias tape to fit the curve as you iron or glue the tape in place. Miter the inner corner of the heart. Fold under the end of the strip, trim the beginning tail and tuck it in the fold for a neat finish.

4. Sew the tape in place using a blind hem or straight stitch (see Chapter 4 – Stitch Samples) when the edges are turned under. If you prefer a more naïve look, use the bias strips with raw edges. Work blanket stitch or a more decorative stitch if desired.

Applying bias tape with fusible web and a mini-iron

Tip: Lightly spray starch the fabric before cutting bias strips and using these tools. This helps to achieve a crisp edge that will hold its shape when the bias tape is being placed and curved on the project.

⊙ Technique 2: reverse appliqué

Reverse appliqué is a technique to consider when trying to appliqué lots of small curved shapes. When dealing with curves in reverse appliqué, you work with the concave curve of the top fabric, which is much easier to manage than the convex outer curves of the appliqué shape, resulting in flatter appliqué.

YOU WILL NEED:
- FREEZER PAPER
- STRAIGHT STITCH FOOT
- DUCK BILL APPLIQUÉ SCISSORS OR SMALL CURVED SCISSORS
- OPEN-TOED APPLIQUÉ FOOT
- MACHINE EMBROIDERY THREAD – RAYON OR COTTON; USE POLYCOTTON IN THE BOBBIN

Use the freezer paper as a stitching guide

Fabric and template assembled to begin reverse appliqué

START STITCHING

1. Trace the appliqué shape on to the dull side of freezer paper and cut it out on the line.
2. Place a piece of contrasting fabric underneath the background fabric, right side up. Pin this piece of fabric securely in place. Put the pins on top of the work so they don't catch. Press the paper shape to the right side of the top fabric.
3. Using the freezer paper as a guide, stitch around the edge of the template with a small, straight stitch using a neutral colored thread or one to match the background fabric.
4. Cut away the inside of the top layer just in from the stitching line with duck bill scissors. This will reveal the lower, contrasting layer of fabric. Take care not to cut the underlying fabric.

Straight stitching (step 3) ready to be covered with satin stitch

5. Using a covering stitch such as satin stitch with stabilizer underneath the work, sew around the raw edge, covering the line of straight stitching. Alternatively, you could use several lines of straight, free motion stitching to give a raw edged look.
6. Tear away the stabilizer and then cut away the excess fabric from around the satin stitch at the back of the work.

7. To make multiple layers of reverse appliqué, follow steps 1 – 4 then repeat these steps again with another colored fabric. Cut away the inside layer of the second appliqué shape, which will now include a portion of the first appliqué shape.

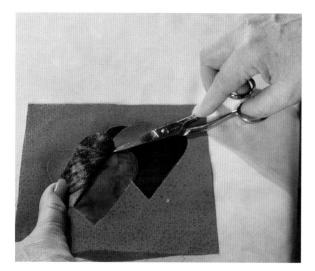

The second cut away includes a portion of the first appliqué shape

8. Cover the raw edges with satin stitch or another decorative stitch. Start by stitching around the first appliqué shape and then stitch the second. When quilting, stitch in the ditch on the inside of the satin stitch to emphasise the reverse appliqué, rather than around the outside as normal.

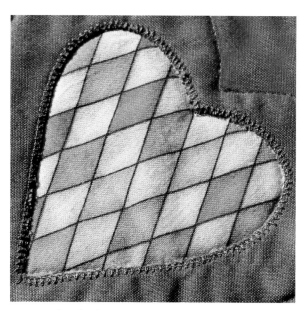

Sample of reverse appliqué with blanket stitch

Technique 3: 3D appliqué

Not all appliquéd shapes need to be attached to the quilt all the way around. It is fun to add some 3D elements that are allowed to 'float' on the quilt surface. There is no limit to how this technique can be used, but 3D appliqué shapes are best added to wall quilts rather than bed quilts.

Sample of 3D appliqué

YOU WILL NEED:
- FUSIBLE WEB
- WATER-SOLUBLE STABILIZER
- MACHINE EMBROIDERY HOOP
- OPEN-TOED APPLIQUÉ FOOT
- MACHINE EMBROIDERY THREAD – USE THE SAME BRAND OF THREAD FOR THE TOP AND BOTTOM, AS BOTH SIDES OF THE WORK CAN BE SEEN

METHOD 1
1. Cut two pieces of fabric large enough for the appliqué shape. Cut two pieces of fusible web slightly smaller than the fabric (to prevent damage to the iron). Iron a piece of fusible web to the back of each piece of fabric. Peel off the paper from the fusible web and press the two pieces together

Love to Machine Appliquét

Appliqué shape satin stitched to water soluble stabilizer

with the right sides of the fabric on the outside. Having two pieces of fusible web in the center of the 'sandwich' gives extra body to the 3D piece. Trace the appliqué shape onto one side of this 'sandwich' and cut it out carefully on the pencil line.

2. Pin the appliqué shape to a piece of water-soluble stabilizer and secure it in a machine embroidery hoop. Use two layers of stabilizer in the hoop for adequate body. Note: The fabric lies flat against the machine bed in a machine embroidery hoop and not on top of the hoop as in hand embroidery.

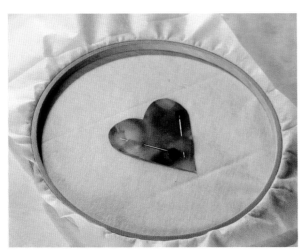

Appliqué shape pinned in place in a machine embroidery hoop

3. Satin stitch around the edge of the appliqué shape. Allow the needle to stitch on the appliqué shape and then stitch just into the water-soluble stabilizer so that the edge of the shape is wrapped with thread. If you are using a thin batting in the center of the appliqué 'sandwich' to give it more body, then this technique is most important so that the white inner layers of fusible web do not show at the edge.

4. Leave a long strand of thread when finishing your work and pull it to the back. Tie a tiny knot in both threads, then thread into a hand needle and pull the ends under the satin stitch on the wrong side to hide the thread.

5. Trim away the excess water-soluble stabilizer and rinse the shape in water to remove all traces of the stabilizer. Refer to the manufacturer's directions to check the temperature of the water to be used. Lay the shapes out on a clean towel to dry. Press when they are dry. They are now ready to be stitched in place after the quilt has been quilted.

METHOD 2

1. Cut two pieces of the same pattern and stitch them with right sides together, leaving an opening for turning. Trim the seam allowance and nick the seam allowances on the curves.

2. Turn the shape to the right side and smooth out any bumps with a knitting needle. Hand stitch the opening closed. Press and attach the shape to the quilt after the quilting has been completed.

Love Affair – A Heart Sampler

Finished size: **48in x 48in (122cm x 122cm)**

Love Affair

– A Heart Sampler

Now it's time to get **practical!**

Caroline has designed *Love Affair – A Heart Sampler* using all the techniques explained in this book. Make the quilt and master the skills required for successful machine appliqué.

> *Methods used:* Freezer paper with glue; Freezer paper without glue; Double-sided fusible web; Facing the shape with water-soluble stabilizer; Bias tape appliqué; Reverse appliqué; 3D appliqué
>
> *Stitches used:* Blind hem stitch, blanket stitch, satin stitch, free motion stitching and grass stitch

MATERIALS:

- 2¼yd (2m) background fabric
- ⅜yd (35cm) striped fabric (Borders 1 and 2)
- An assortment of print fabrics as listed in the table on page 32 (hearts)
- ⅝yd (50cm) striped fabric (bias binding).
  You will need only ⅜yd (30cm) fabric for the binding if it is not cut on the bias **or** ¼in iron-on purchased pre-made bias tape in a color to suit the fabrics.
- Batting at least 56in x 56in (140cm x 140cm)
- 3yd (2.8m) backing fabric
- Double-sided fusible web
- Freezer paper
- Water-soluble stabilizer
- Iron-on fabric stabilizer
- Small amount of nylon net
- Template plastic
- Monofilament thread (appliqué)

- Lightweight bobbin thread or polyester thread to match the background fabric (bobbin)
- Rayon machine embroidery threads to match the appliqué fabrics
- Jeans needles – 70/10 and 80/12
- Machine embroidery needle – 90/14
- Twin needle – 2.0/80
- Flat end appliqué pins
- Small kebab stick
- Scissors – fabric, paper and sharp embroidery scissors
- ¼in bias tape maker
- Machine embroidery hoop
- Glue stick suitable for use on fabrics
- Sewing machine with open-toed appliqué foot, ¼in foot, darning foot and the ability to drop or cover the feed dogs
- General sewing supplies

Quilt Layout Diagram

Heart Number	Heart Template	Fabric	Yardage (metric)
1, 2	A	Pink floral	8in x 16in (20cm x 40cm)
3, 4	A	Green floral	8in x 16in (20cm x 40cm)
5, 7	B	Green floral	4in x 8in (10cm x 20cm)
6, 8	B	Pink floral	4in x 8in (10cm x 20cm)
9, 10 11, 12	C	Purple tone-on-tone	¼yd (20cm)
13, 14	D	Green tone-on-tone	8in x 16in (20cm x 40cm)
15, 18	B	Pink tone-on-tone	4in x 8in (10cm x 20cm)
16, 17	B	Pink tone-on-tone	4in x 8in (10cm x 20cm)
19, 20	A	Dark pink	8in x 16in (20cm x 40cm)
	B	Pink floral/ green floral	4in x 16in (10cm x 40cm)
21, 22	B	Pink floral	4in x 8in (10cm x 20cm)
23, 24	B	Pink tone-on-tone	4in x 8in (10cm x 20cm)
25, 26	B	Green floral	4in x 8in (10cm x 20cm)

Template usage and fabric requirements for each heart in **Love Affair**

CUTTING:

From the background fabric, cut:
- One strip, 18in x width of fabric. From it, cut one square, 18in (center block). Trim the remaining part of the strip to 10in wide (Border 3).
- One strip, 17in x width of fabric. Crosscut into two squares, 17in. Cut each square once on the diagonal to yield four half-square triangles (center block setting triangles).
- Four strips, 10in x width of fabric (Border 3)

From the striped fabric for Borders 1 and 2, cut:
- Eight strips, 1½in x width of fabric

PREPARATION:

Trace Hearts A and B from page 39 on to template plastic. Cut out each heart carefully and accurately on the line. Make the edges as smooth as possible. Label each heart.

MAKE THE CENTER BLOCK:

Fold the 18in square of background fabric twice on the diagonal and lightly finger press to crease. These diagonals will assist with the placement of the hearts. Refer to the Quilt Layout Diagram to see where each heart is placed.

Heart 1

HEARTS 1 – 2

Method used: *Freezer paper with glue*

Stitch used: *Blind hem stitch*

1. Trace around the Heart A template twice on the dull side of the freezer paper. Cut out the hearts on the pencil line.

2. Refer to the instructions for the Freezer Paper with Glue method on page 12 as you work on the following steps.

3. With a dry iron, press the shiny side of the freezer paper to the wrong side of the pink floral fabric. Cut the fabric heart out adding a ¼in seam allowance. Clip the inner curves and center dip. Add glue to the edges of the freezer paper template and the fabric seam allowance. Roll the seam allowance over the freezer paper.

4. Once the glue has dried, pin the heart in place on the center square, with the pins perpendicular to the edge. The point of the heart should be about 1in from the center of the block, and the point and dip of the heart should lie on one of the finger pressed creases.

5. Blind hem stitch in place with monofilament thread, removing the pins as you come to them. (See Chapter 4.)

6. Repeat this process for Heart 2. Alternatively, you could practise the Freezer Paper without Glue method on Heart 2. (See Chapter 2.)

Heart 3

HEARTS 3 – 4

Method used: *Face the shape with water-soluble stabilizer*

Stitch used: *Blind hem stitch*

1. Trace around the Heart A template twice on the water-soluble stabilizer using a water-erasable pen or a pencil.

2. Refer to the instructions for Facing the Shape with Water-soluble Stabilizer method on page 15 as you work on the following steps.

3. Pin the stabilizer on to the green floral fabric. Stitch around the shape on the line with a small straight stitch and matching thread. Cut out the heart adding a ¼in seam allowance. Cut small nicks into the seam allowance; cut a slit in the water-soluble stabilizer. Turn the heart right side out.

4. Pin Heart 3 in place on the center square, with the point about 1in from the center of the block, and the point and dip on the diagonal crease. Blind hem stitch in place using monofilament thread. (See Chapter 4.)

5. Prepare Heart 4 using any of the methods trialled. Stitch it in place diagonally opposite Heart 3 using blind hem stitch.

Heart 5

HEARTS 5 – 8

Method used: *Double-sided fusible web*

Stitch used: *Blanket stitch*

1. Trace around the Heart B template four times on the paper backing of a lightweight fusible web. Cut the hearts out leaving approximately ¼in seam allowance around each shape.

2. Refer to the instructions for the Double-sided fusible web method on page 16 as you work on the following steps.

3. Fuse two hearts to the wrong side of the green floral fabric and two hearts to the wrong side of the pink floral fabric. Cut the hearts out on the pencil line and peel off the paper.

Heart 9 stitched with satin stitch

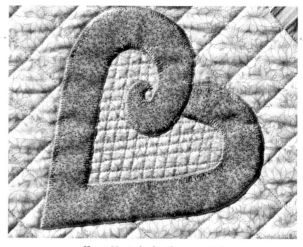

Heart 11 stitched with grass stitch

4. Place the two green floral hearts ½in above the large pink floral hearts already in place. Place the small pink floral hearts ½in above the large green floral hearts. Once you are happy with the arrangement, fuse the hearts in place.

5. Blanket stitch around them using rayon machine embroidery thread to highlight the stitching. Refer to the instructions for blanket stitch on page 22.

6. When each heart is complete, pull the threads to the back of the work and tie them off.

Once the center block is completed, trim it back to 17½in square with the appliqué centered.

ADD BORDER 1:

Note: *If you are using a striped fabric for Border 1, the best finish is to miter the corners. If you are not using a striped fabric, then you can miter the corners or choose to finish the border with straight corners.*

Referring to the instructions for Borders with Mitered Corners on page 94, add Border 1 using four of the 1½in strips of striped fabric. Press the seams towards the border.

> Tip: Make sure the same colored stripe is located at the centre of each side to ensure that all four mitred corners look alike.

ADD THE SETTING TRIANGLES WITH HEARTS 9 – 12

Method used: *Double-sided fusible web*
Stitches used: *Satin stitch for Hearts 9 and 11 and grass stitch for Hearts 10 and 12*

1. Pin, then sew the background fabric setting triangles to each side of the center square. The triangles have been cut so that their corners will overlap. This will create an effect where Border 1 appears to be 'floating' on the background fabric.

2. Trace four Heart C (both inner and outer lines) on to the paper side of double-sided fusible web. Cut out each heart with a seam allowance of approximately ¼in. Note that the pattern has already been reversed, so it can be traced directly on to the fusible web.

3. Refer to the instructions for the Double-sided fusible web method on page 16 as you work on the following steps.

4. Peel the backing paper off the four hearts and fuse them on to the wrong side of the purple tone-on-tone fabric. Cut out each heart on the drawn line.

5. Place a heart on each setting triangle with the tip 8in from the straight edge of the triangle (see Diagram 1). Once you are happy with the placement, fuse each heart in place.

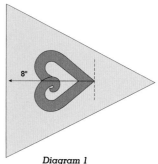

Diagram 1

6. Draw a faint pencil line on the heart to continue the overlapping curl at the top of the shape. This is stitched when the appliqué is sewn to give a smooth, continuous line (see Diagram 2).

Pencil in the sewing line

Diagram 2

7. Satin stitch two diagonally opposite hearts (Hearts 9 and 11) in place – remembering to use stabilizer behind the work – using contrasting rayon machine embroidery thread. Refer to the instructions for satin stitch on page 20.

8. Grass stitch the two remaining hearts (Hearts 10 and 12), again remembering to use stabilizer behind the work. Refer to the instructions for Grass stitch on page 22. Use the same thread that you used for satin stitching Hearts 9 and 11 to help visually tie the four hearts in the setting triangles together.

9. Once the appliqué is completed, trim the quilt top to 29¼in square, centering the design.

Tip: If an appliqué shape is difficult to cut from template plastic, it is best to trace the shape directly on to the fusible web to ensure accuracy.

ADD BORDER 2

Referring to the instructions for Borders with Mitered Corners on page 94, add Border 2 using four of the 1½in strips of striped fabric. Press the seams towards the border.

Tip: For beginners, it is easier to use threads that match the appliqué fabric, so that any minor faults will not show up so readily.

BORDER 3

1. Join the five 10in strips of background fabric end to end to make one long strip.

2. Measure the length of the quilt through the center. Cut two strips this length plus 1in from the long strip for the left and right borders. The extra length will be trimmed once the appliqué is completed.

HEARTS 13 – 14

Heart 13 (green) with Hearts 15 and 16 (pink) on Border 3

Method used: *Double-sided fusible web*
Stitches used: *Free motion straight stitch (inner edge) and sketchy free motion stitch (outer edge)*

1. Trace two Heart D (both inner and outer lines) on to the paper side of double-sided fusible web. Cut each heart out adding a seam allowance of approximately ¼in. The shape is symmetrical, so there are no problems with mirror imaging.

2. Refer to the instructions for the Double-sided Fusible Web method on page 16 as you work on the following steps.

3. Fuse the hearts to the wrong side of the green tone-on-tone fabric. Cut out each heart on the drawn line and peel the backing paper off them.

4. Place a heart in the center of each of the border strips that you have cut, with their points 2in from the raw edge. Once you are happy with the placement, press the hearts in place.

5. Free motion straight stitch the inner edge of each heart. Begin by using a rayon machine embroidery thread that matches the green tone-on-tone fabric (although note that the bright quilt uses a contrasting thread here). Refer to the instructions for Free Motion stitching on page 23 and remember to add a stabilizer behind the work.

6. Free motion straight stitch with a sketchy look around the outer edge of each heart using rayon machine embroidery threads in two shades of the one color. Refer to the instructions for Free Motion Stitching on page 23. Start sewing at the bottom of the heart and work up to the center of the top on one side. Then repeat with the other side of the heart (see Diagram 3).

Diagram 3

HEARTS 15 – 18

Method used: *Twin needling*

Stitch used: *Feather stitch*

1. Trace four Heart B on to the paper side of double-sided fusible web. Cut out each heart leaving a seam allowance of approximately ¼in around the shapes.

2. Refer to the instructions for the Double-sided Fusible Web method on page 16 as you work on the following steps.

3. Fuse the hearts to the wrong side of the pink tone-on-tone fabric. Cut out each heart on the drawn line and peel off the backing paper.

Heart 15 (next to Heart 13 on Border 3)

4. Place a heart on either side of the lower edge of Hearts 13 and 14 (see Diagram 4). Fuse the hearts in place.

5. Do a test with scrap fabric to determine if you need to use a lightweight iron-on interfacing as a stabilizer behind the work. This will depend on your machine.

Edge of border

2"

Diagram 4

6. Twin needle the hearts in place using feather stitch worked with two shades of rayon machine embroidery thread. This will emphasise the stitching. Refer to the instructions for Twin Needling on page 24.

7. Pull the threads to the back and tie them off.

8. Trim the border strips so that they are exactly the same length as the quilt, keeping the appliquéd hearts centered. Pin, then sew the strips to the left and right edges of the quilt with the points of the hearts closer to the quilt center.

> **Tip:** Start the stitching on your hearts from the bottom of the shape, working right around it. This will enable you to control the stitching on the lower point without it becoming too messy.

Heart 19

HEARTS 19 — 20

Method used: *Bias tape appliqué*

Stitch used: *Blind hem stitch or straight stitch*

1. Measure the width of the quilt through the center. From the long strip of background fabric, cut two strips to this length plus 1in for the top and bottom borders.

2. Cut four bias strips of fabric the width required for your preferred method of bias tape making.

3. Trace around the Heart A template twice and the Heart B template four times on the paper side of lightweight fusible web. Cut each heart out leaving a ¼in seam allowance.

4. Fuse the large A hearts to the wrong side of the dark pink fabric, two of the B hearts to the wrong side of the pink floral fabric and two B hearts to the wrong side of the green floral fabric. Cut out each heart on the line.

5. Refer to the instructions for the Double-sided Fusible Web method on page 16 as you work on the following steps.

6. Before peeling the paper from the back of the fusible web and fusing the hearts in place on the border strips, lay the hearts out as they will appear on the quilt. Use the quilt photo and Diagram 5 as a guide. Lift the hearts slightly, pencil in the overlap and trim away the excess fabric on the small green floral heart. Repeat this process for the dark pink heart noting where the small pink floral heart will shadow it when it is laid on top.

7. Remove the backing paper from the hearts. Place them in a group in the center of the border strips (see Diagram 5). Once you are happy with the placement, fuse the hearts in place.

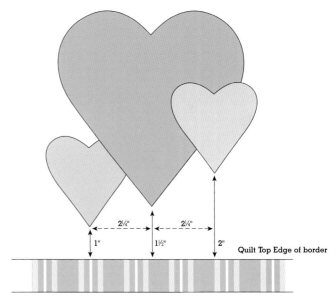

Diagram 5

> **Tip:** If you use at least ³⁄₈yd (35cm) of fabric to cut these bias strips, you will not need to join them.

8. Apply the bias tape using the method of your choice with a blind hem stitch or a straight stitch worked in a matching thread. Refer to the instructions for bias tape appliqué on page 25 and blind hem stitch on page 19. Start with the lower green floral small heart, mitering the bias tape at the inner top center of the heart as you go. The large heart is next, with the bias tape covering the raw edges of the bias tape on the green heart. The small pink floral heart is done last, with its bias tape covering the start and finish of the bias tape on the large heart. For a neat finish, tuck under and press the raw edge on the end of the bias tape before completing the stitching on the small pink floral heart.

9. Trim the border strips so that they are exactly the same width as the quilt, keeping the appliquéd hearts centered. Pin, then sew the strips to the top and bottom edges of the quilt with the points of the hearts closer to the quilt center. There will be very little further shrinkage due to appliqué and positioning hearts 21 – 24 is easier when the borders are in place.

Heart 21

HEARTS 21 – 22
Method used: *Reverse appliqué*
Stitch used: *Satin stitch*

1. Lightly trace around the Heart B template on two diagonally opposite corners of Border 3 with a retractable pencil (see Diagram 6).

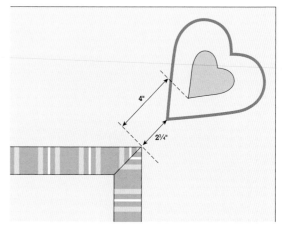

Diagram 6

2. Refer to the instructions for the Reverse Appliqué method on page 27 as you work on the following steps.

3. Cut two pieces of pink floral fabric large enough to comfortably cover the B Heart. Position them under the hearts you traced on two corners of Border 3.

4. Using the pencil line as a guide, stitch around the edge of the heart shapes with a straight stitch and neutral thread. Cut away the Border 3 fabric inside the sewn heart with duck bill scissors to reveal the pink floral fabric underneath.

5. Satin stitch around the heart using a contrasting thread.

6. Centre the Heart A template over the small pink floral reverse appliquéd heart and trace lightly with a pencil. Add a long curved satin stitched line from the point of the heart. For accuracy, use a freezer paper template. Draw the line twice for each corner from the tip of the hearts. Satin stitch this line for a decorative effect. Don't forget the stabilizer.

Love to Machine Appliqué

Heart 23 and 24

HEARTS 23 – 26

Method used: *3D appliqué*

Stitch used: *Satin stitch*

Note: *These hearts are not attached to the quilt until all the quilting is completed.*

1. Refer to the instructions for the Reverse Appliqué method on page 27 as you work on the following steps.

2. Cut 2 rectangles, 11½in x 6½in from the pink floral fabric. Back each piece of fabric with fusible web.

3. Remove the paper backing and fuse the two pieces of fabric together to create a 'sandwich'. The fabric on both sides should be right side out.

4. Trace two small B Hearts on one side of the 'sandwich' and cut them out carefully on the line.

5. Repeat Steps 2 – 4 with the green floral fabric to make another two heart 'sandwiches'.

6. Satin stitch around each of the four hearts.

7. When the quilting is completed on the quilt, use a small straight stitch with monofilament thread or a matching rayon thread, and stitch just inside the satin stitch only at the top of the hearts. Refer to the quilt photo for placement.

8. Satin stitch the long curved line coming from the lower edge of the 3D hearts closest to the center.

QUILTING AND BINDING:

1. Press the quilt top ready for quilting and binding. Cut the length of backing fabric in half. Remove the selvages and join the two lengths down a long edge.

2. Referring to Preparing the Quilt Top for Quilting in General Quiltmaking Instructions on page 94, layer the backing , batting and quilt ready for quilting. Pin baste.

3. Quilt as desired. *Love Affair* was professionally quilted by Larraine Smith.

4. Bind the quilt with the striped fabric strips, referring to Binding in General Quiltmaking Instructions, page 94.

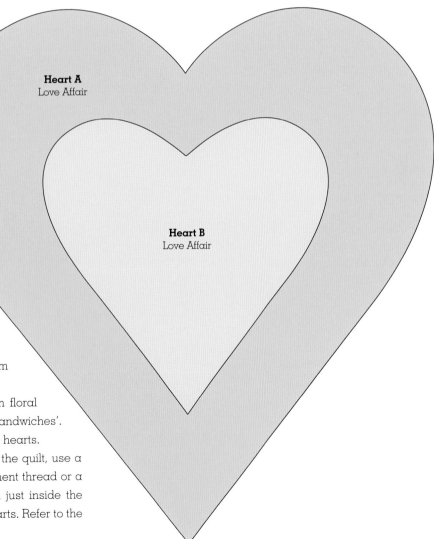

Heart A
Love Affair

Heart B
Love Affair

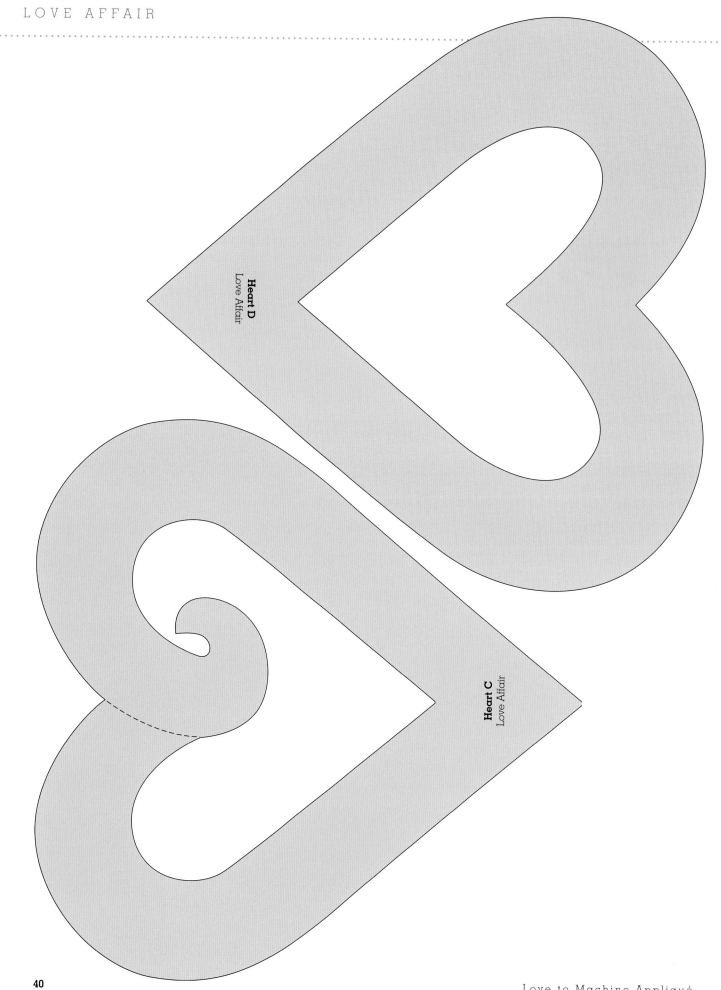

Heart D
Love Affair

Heart C
Love Affair

Love to Machine Appliqué

Love Affair - A Heart Sampler Quilt *using bright colors*

Love Affair - **A Heart Sampler** *Quilt Layout Diagram*

Love Affair - Bright Colors

Here is another version of *Love Affair* – another chance to practise all the techniques necessary for successful machine appliqué. The fabrics used are strong and vibrant reflecting the colors in the stunning stripe used to emphasize the design.

Heart Number	Heart Template	Fabric	Yardage *(Metric)*
1, 2	A	Red tone-on-tone	8in x 16in *(20cm x 40cm)*
3, 4	A	Yellow hand dyed	8in x 16in *(20cm x 40cm)*
5, 7	B	Green spot	4in x 8in *(10cm x 20cm)*
6, 8	B	Multi stripe	4in x 8in *(10cm x 20cm)*
9, 10, 11, 12	C	Red spot	¼yd *(20cm)*
13, 14	D	Light green	8in x 16in *(20cm x 40cm)*
15, 18	B	Orange check	4in x 8in *(10cm x 20cm)*
16, 17	B	Orange swirl	4in x 8in *(10cm x 20cm)*
19, 20	A	Yellow spot	8in x 16in *(20cm x 40cm)*
	B	Purple	4in x 16in *(10cm x 40cm)*
21, 22	B	Multi diamond	4in x 8in *(10cm x 20cm)*
23, 24	B	Yellow spot	4in x 8in *(10cm x 20cm)*
25, 26	B	Orange spot	4in x 8in *(10cm x 20cm)*

Clementine Vines

Finished size: 62½in x 70½in (160cm x 180cm)

Clementine Vines

This appealing **strippy-style** quilt is the perfect
way to show off a favorite **floral fabric** that you just can't bear
to cut into small patches. Pick up colors from the
feature fabric when choosing fabrics for the appliqué.

Method used: Freezer paper; bias tape appliqué

Stitch used: Blind hem stitch

MATERIALS:

- 2⅛yd (1.9m) floral print fabric (sashings and Border 2)
- 1⅝yd (1.45m) yellow and white striped fabric (background)
- ⅝yd (50cm) green tone-on-tone fabric (bias stems)
- Fat eighth of five different red tone-on-tone print fabrics (flowers)
- Scraps of green fabrics at least 3½in x 7in (leaves and calyxes)
- ⅞yd (80cm) red tone-on-tone print fabric (Border 1 and binding)
- 4yd (3.5m) backing fabric
- Batting at least 67in x 75in (170cm x 190cm)
- Fabric stabilizer
- Freezer paper and Chinagraph pencil (or equivalent)
- Glue stick suitable for use on fabric

- Spray starch
- ¼in bias maker (optional)
- Tailor's awl or bamboo skewer
- Spray water bottle
- Green rayon or cotton machine embroidery threads (leaf veins)
- Monofilament thread (appliqué and quilting)
- Polyester thread to match the floral and background fabrics (quilting)
- Size 70/10 jeans needle or 60/8 universal needle
- Rotary cutter, ruler and mat
- Sewing machine
- General sewing supplies

From the floral print fabric, cut:

- Five strips, 4½in x width of fabric (sashings)
- Seven strips, 6½in x width of fabric (Border 2)

From the yellow and white striped fabric, cut:

- Four strips, 9½in down the **length** of the fabric. Trim them to 56½in long.

From the yardage of red tone-on-tone print fabric, cut:

- Six strips, 1½in x width of fabric (Border 1)
- Seven strips, 2¼in x width of fabric (binding)

Spray the green tone-on-tone print fabric lightly with starch.

From the green tone-on-tone print fabric, cut:

- 11 strips, ½in wide on the bias. If you are not using a ¼in bias maker, cut your bias strips the appropriate width to make strips that will finish ¼in wide when appliquéd to the quilt.

PREPARATION

1. Trace the shape for the curve of the vine from page 47 on to freezer paper. Cut it out carefully. Fold it in half to mark the center, as indicated on the pattern.

2. Fold each of the strips of yellow and white fabric in half, long edges matching, and press lightly to crease. Then fold them in half with short edges matching, and press lightly to crease.

3. Place the vine template on a yellow and white strip with the straight edge sitting on the center crease and the center of the template aligned with the center of the strip (see Diagram 1). Iron the freezer paper in place. Trace around the curved edge lightly with a pencil.

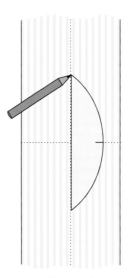

Diagram 1

4. Lift the freezer paper off the fabric and turn it 180 degrees. Position it back on the fabric with the straight edge on the center crease of the fabric, and the top of the template matching the bottom of the line you just traced (see Diagram 2). Again, trace lightly around the curved edge.

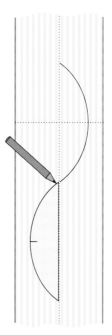

Diagram 2

5. Continue working in this manner, placing the curve of the template alternately to the left and right of the center crease and tracing it to create a continuous curve down the length of each strip of yellow and white fabric.

6. Trace eight large leaves, eight medium leaves and eight small leaves on to the dull side of the freezer paper. Then trace another eight large leaves, eight medium leaves and eight small leaves on to the shiny side of the freezer paper – you will need to use a Chinagraph pencil or equivalent to do this.

7. Trace the shapes for the flower and calyx on to the dull side of the freezer paper 16 times.

> Tip: Using a Chinagraph or similar pencil to trace appliqué shapes on to the shiny side of the freezer paper is a quick and easy way of creating reversed appliqué shapes. It avoids the needs to trace shapes on to paper and then use a light box or window to trace them in reverse.

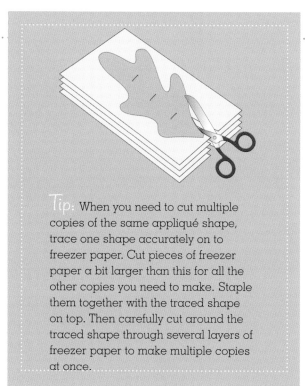

Tip: When you need to cut multiple copies of the same appliqué shape, trace one shape accurately on to freezer paper. Cut pieces of freezer paper a bit larger than this for all the other copies you need to make. Staple them together with the traced shape on top. Then carefully cut around the traced shape through several layers of freezer paper to make multiple copies at once.

8. Prepare the leaves, flowers and calyxes for appliqué, referring to the instructions for the Freezer Paper with Glue method on page 12. Note that when you cut the flower shapes, you will need to add ¼in along the bottom edge to sit under the calyx. This seam allowance is not glued to the freezer paper but will sit flat under the calyx.

COMPLETE THE APPLIQUÉ

1. Join the green bias strips end to end to make one long strip. Press the seams open and trim them so that they are even with the edges of the strip. Use a bias maker or your preferred method to turn under the edges of this strip ready for appliqué.

2. Cut the long strip into four equal lengths. Pin or glue each length in place on a yellow and white strip of fabric. The centre of the strip should sit on the traced line.

3. Referring to the instructions for blind hem stitch on page 19, appliqué the vines in place.

4. Referring to the photograph of the quilt for guidance, pin the flowers and calyxes in place in the center of each vine 'valley'. Blind hem stitch them in place.

5. Pin the leaves in place, scattering them randomly over the four strips. Blind hem stitch them in place.

6. Spray water on all the appliqué shapes, then remove the freezer paper from behind them .

Tip: Occasionally you may find – to your horror – that the glue you have used to temporarily attach your appliqué shapes to the background fabric has the effect of making the fabric dye run when you wet the fabric in order to remove the freezer paper. This can occur even after you've prewashed your fabrics. It's a good idea to have on hand a product such as Dylon Color Safe Run Away, which removes color stains caused by dye runs.

FINISH THE QUILT

1. Join the 4½in strips of floral fabric cut for the sashings end to end to make one long strip. From this long strip cut three strips each 56½in long.

2. Referring to the photograph for guidance, lay out the four appliquéd strips and the three floral strips. Sew them together along their long edges. Press.

3. Join the 1½in strips of red tone-on-tone fabric end to end to make one long strip. Measure your quilt vertically through the center and trim two strips this length from the long strip. Sew them to the left and right edges of the quilt.

4. Measure your quilt horizontally through the center and trim two strips this length from the remainder of the long strip. Sew them to the top and bottom edges of the quilt.

5. Join the 6½in strips of floral fabric cut for Border 2 end to end to make one long strip. Repeat steps 3 and 4 to add Border 2 to your quilt.

6. Satin stitch a vein on each leaf. To do this, attach fabric stabilizer behind each leaf, and stitch with a variety of green machine embroidery threads. Caroline started each vein with a stitch width of 2, tapering off to a width of just under 1, curving the vein as she went.

7. Press your quilt top ready for quilting and binding. Referring to Preparing the Quilt Top for Quilting in General Quiltmaking Instructions, page 94, layer the backing, batting and quilt ready for quilting. Pin baste.

8. Quilt as desired. *Clementine Vines* was machine quilted by Larraine Smith of Mudgee, Australia. She stitched around the leaves and vines using monofilament thread. She then worked wonderful loose feathers and swirls on the floral fabric with a red variegated thread, and vine-like swirls on the striped background fabric with yellow cotton thread.

9. Join the seven strips cut for the binding end to end to make one long strip. Use it to bind the quilt, referring to Binding in General Quiltmaking Instructions, page 94.

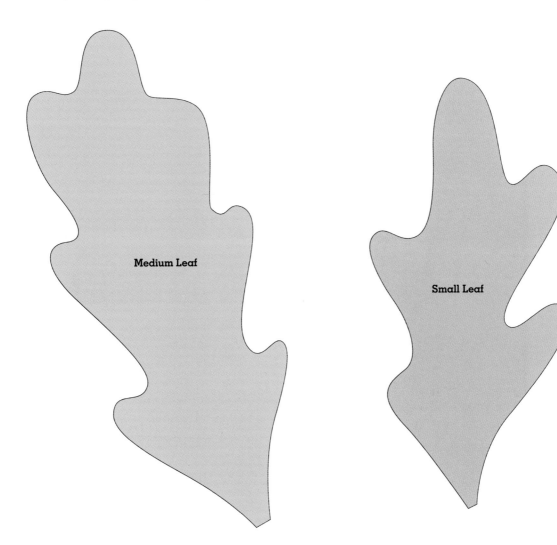

Medium Leaf

Small Leaf

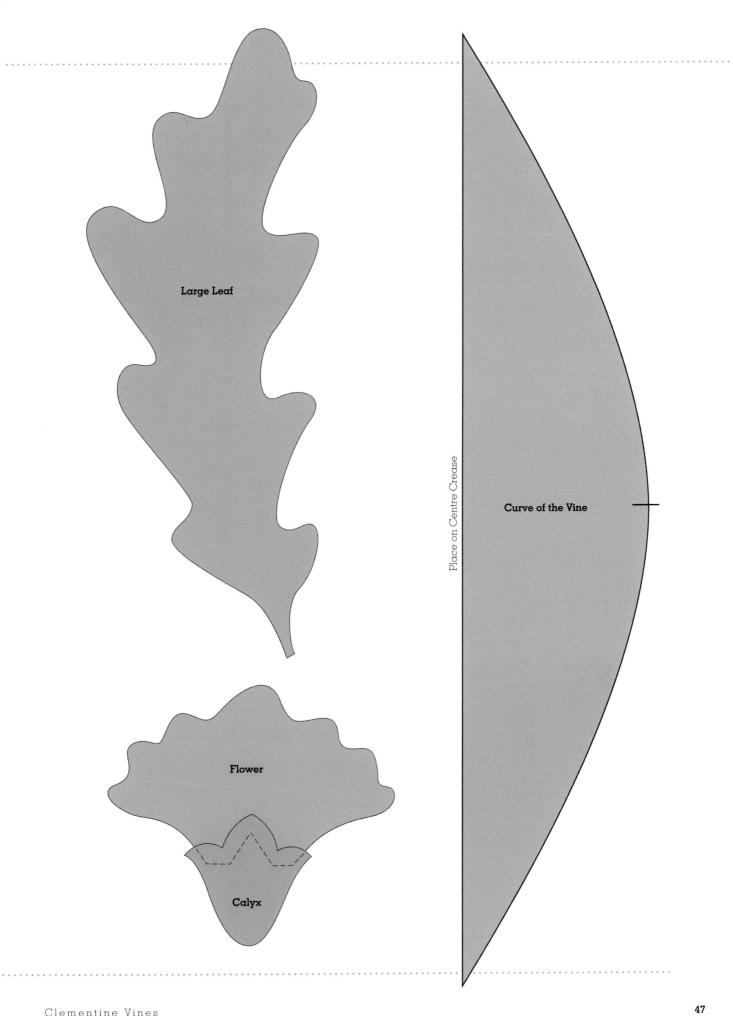

Large Leaf

Place on Centre Crease

Curve of the Vine

Flower

Calyx

Autumn Leaves

Finished size: 37½in x 44in (95cm x 112cm)

Love to Machine Quilt

Autumn Leaves

Mother Nature puts on a wonderful display of
color every year during fall.
Leaves in a myriad of shades of brown, orange,
russet, yellow, green and red tumble from this
wallhanging to celebrate the magic of this season.

> Method used: Double-sided fusible web;
> 3D appliqué
> Stitches used: Satin stitch; free motion stitching

MATERIALS:

- 1⅜yd (1.3m) mottled green fabric (background and Border 2)
- ½yd (50cm) mottled mustard fabric (Border 1 and binding)
- 6in (15cm) squares of hand dyed and print fabrics in a range of fall colors (leaves)
- ⅞yd (65cm) water-soluble stabilizer
- ¼yd (15cm) of tulle, net and/or organza in fall colors (leaves)
- 1⅜yd (1.3m) backing fabric
- Batting at least 42in x 48in (105cm x 122cm)
- Double-sided fusible web
- Iron-on tear away fabric stabilizer
- Template plastic
- Machine embroidery hoop
- Permanent felt tipped marking pen
- Machine embroidery threads in fall tones to match the leaf fabrics
- Monofilament thread
- Lightweight bobbin thread
- Top stitch or embroidery needle for sewing machine
- Pressing cloth
- Spray starch
- Rotary cutter, ruler and mat
- Sewing machine with open toed appliqué foot and quilting foot
- General sewing supplies

PREPARATION:

1. Use spray starch in keeping with the manufacturer's instructions to starch the green and mustard mottled fabrics. This will give added body to the quilt top before you begin to appliqué.
2. Trace the leaf from page 52 on to template plastic using the permanent marking pen. Cut it out accurately. Mark the front of the template.
3. Use the template to trace 37 leaves on to the paper side of the fusible web, leaving ½in between shapes. Reverse the template for some of the leaves.

CUTTING:

From the green mottled fabric, cut:

- Two strips, 5in x width of fabric (Border 2)
- One strip, 35in x width of fabric. From it cut one strip, 26½in x 33in (quilt center) and two strips, 5in x 35in (Border 2).

From the mottled mustard fabric, cut:

- Four strips, 1½in x width of fabric (Border 1)
- Four strips, 2¼in x width of fabric (binding)

ASSEMBLE THE QUILT

1. In this project, the borders are added to the quilt center before the appliqué. This is because some of the leaves are stitched over the seam lines, extending into the borders.

2. Begin by trimming two of the 1½in mottled mustard strips to 33in. Sew them to the left and right edges of the quilt center. Press seams away from the quilt center.

3. Trim the remaining two 1½in mottled mustard strips to 28½in. Sew them to the top and bottom edges of the quilt, and press as before.

4. Sew the 35in strips of mottled green fabric to the left and right edges of the quilt. Trim the remaining two strips of mottled green fabric to 37½in and sew them to the top and bottom edges of the quilt.

5. Press iron-on stabilizer on to the wrong side of the quilt.

SATIN STITCH APPLIQUÉ

1. Cut out all the leaves that you traced on to fusible web about ¼in outside the traced lines. Fuse the shapes to the wrong side of the 6in squares of assorted print fabrics. Then cut each leaf out accurately on the line.

2. Lay out all the leaves on the quilt, referring to the photograph for guidance. Bear in mind that a dozen or more 3D leaves will be added in the next stage, so leave some gaps for the net or organza leaves. They look very effective when they overlap satin stitched appliquéd leaves.

> Tip: If you have a digital or Polaroid camera, take a photograph of your arrangement at this stage. It will be a valuable point of reference, and will mean that you can remove most of the leaves from the quilt and work on just a small section at a time.

3. Remove the backing paper from the leaves, and fuse three or four together in a group to the quilt.

4. Refer to the instructions for satin stitch on page 20 as you work on the following steps, paying particular attention to sewing curves and points.

5. If your leaves overlap, start by stitching the leaf on the lowest layer – the one that is overlapped by others, but doesn't overlap anything itself. The stitching can commence with a small straight stitch just on the edge of the leaf, which will be covered later by satin stitch. This has the effect of locking the stitching. If your first leaf is overlapped by others, it may even be the case that you commence this straight stitching on the overlapping leaf.

6. When you complete the stitching on the last leaf in the group, you may find that you can't finish with some small straight locking stitches. If not, take both threads to the back of the work and tie off securely.

7. As you complete each group of three or four leaves, refer to the photograph you have taken of your preferred arrangement to add another group of leaves to the quilt. Working in small batches like this prevents the edges of the leaves from fraying before you stitch them.

3D APPLIQUÉ

1. Cut two pieces of fusible web, each 5⅞ in square. Fuse each of them to the wrong side of a 6in square of hand dyed or print fabric. Remove the backing paper, then fuse the squares to each other, wrong sides together.

2. Use the template to trace a leaf on one side of the fabric square. Cut the shape out carefully on the traced line.

3. Refer to the instructions for 3D Appliqué on page 28 to complete the leaf. Be careful not to sew off the points of the leaf too much, as the thread may unravel when the water soluble stabilizer is rinsed away.

4. Repeat to make a total of eight 3D leaves.

5. There are a several ways of attaching these leaves to your quilt. One is by stitching the veins. If this is your preferred method, put your leaves aside. Another way is to attach the leaf just at the top edges. If this is your preferred method, embroider the vein details on the leaf now before removing the leaf from the hoop. Once the quilting is completed, this leaf can be sewn in place using either invisible monofilament thread or a matching machine embroidery thread.

6. Trim away the excess water-soluble stabilizer and rinse the leaf as described on page 29.

TULLE AND ORGANZA LEAVES

1. Leaves made using tulle, net or organza as their base are made in a manner slightly different to the 3D technique. Start by cutting a piece of water-soluble stabilizer and a piece of tulle, net or organza large enough to fit into the embroidery hoop.

2. Use the leaf template to trace the leaf shape onto the stabilizer using a permanent marking pen. Pin the tulle, net or organza on top of the tracing.

3. Straight stitch around the outside edge of the leaf using free motion stitching as described on page 23. Caroline recommends stitching this line twice. You can use the same thread in the top of the machine and the bobbin, or you can vary them. If you decide to vary them, Caroline recommends using the same brand and thickness of thread to avoid any problems with thread tension.

4. Stitch in from the outside edge as shown in Diagram 1. Caroline likes to do this in a series of 'runs': the first run follows the direction of the pencil lines. On the second run, she works with the same thread to fill in the gaps between stitches and varies the length of the lines of stitching. On the third run, she changes the thread color, and works some additional stitching on top of the first two runs. Caroline finds that this variation in thread color gives a more natural and dimensional look to the leaf. Make 10 tulle or organza leaves for this project.

Diagram 1

5. Again, you have a choice about how these leaves are attached once the quilting has been completed. If they are only to be attached at the top edges, embroider the veins at this stage.

6. Remove the hoop and trim away the excess tulle, net or organza and water-soluble stabilizer. Then rinse to remove the stabilizer. Trim the tulle, net or organza back to the stitched edge of the leaf.

FINISH THE QUILT

1. Press your quilt top ready for quilting and binding. Referring to Preparing the Quilt Top for Quilting in General Quiltmaking Instructions, page 94, layer the backing, batting and quilt ready for quilting. Pin baste.

2. Quilt as desired. *Autumn Leaves* was machine quilted by Caroline. She stitched around all of the satin stitched leaves and in the ditch of Border 1 using monofilament thread. Using rayon thread, she then quilted the vein lines of the satin stitched leaves. A variegated rayon machine embroidery thread was used to work leaf shapes in Border 2. To maintain continuity, a meandering loop design was quilted from one leaf to the next.

3. Pin the 3D and tulle, net or organza leaves in place on the quilt. Those on which you have already embroidered the veins are attached with a row of stitching along the top edges using thread to match the satin stitching. The remaining leaves can be stitched in place by embroidering the veins.

4. Join the four strips cut for the binding end to end to make one long strip. Use it to bind the quilt, referring to Binding in General Quiltmaking Instructions, page 94.

5. Finally stitch any leaves in place that overhang the edges of the quilt.

Leaf

Delightful Dahlias

Wowee! These big, bright dahlias are reminiscent of
hot summer days. With many individual shapes to be cut and fused,
there is quite a bit of preparation involved in this project,
but the end results are worth it. Choose hand dyed fabrics
in luscious shades and bring your flowers to life.

> Method used: Double-sided fusible web
>
> Stitch used: Free motion stitching

Delightful Dahlias

Finished size: 42in x 37in (107cm x 94cm)

MATERIALS:

- 1½yd (1.25m) mottled dark blue fabric (background and binding)
- Sets of three 12in (30cm) squares of hand dyed fabric. The squares in each set should be different values – very light, light and medium – of the same color (large flowers). Caroline used pinks, yellow and oranges in her quilt. You will need six sets of squares to make six large flowers. See Tip.
- Sets of three 10in (25cm) squares of hand dyed fabric. The squares in these sets should be one light and two medium of the same color (small flowers). You will need 10 sets of squares to make 10 small flowers. See Tip.
- 1¼yd (1.2m) backing fabric
- Batting at least 41in x 46in (104cm x 117cm)
- Double-sided fusible web
- Iron-on tear away fabric stabilizer (optional)
- Freezer paper
- Teflon coated appliqué mat
- Tulle or net to use as a stabilizer
- White pencil or chalk pencil
- Compass
- Machine embroidery threads to match appliqué fabrics
- Monofilament thread (quilting)
- Dark blue metallic thread (quilting)
- Jeans 12/80 or top stitch needle
- 90/14 or 100/16 needle
- Light box (optional)
- Rotary cutter, ruler and mat
- Sewing machine with free motion quilting foot
- General sewing supplies

Tip: Select fabrics for your flowers that don't fray readily. Requirements for these fabrics shown in the Materials list are a guide only. Caroline used the same fabrics in more than one flower, changing their position – sometimes the lightest value fabric was the bottom layer of the appliqué, sometimes it was the top layer. The fabric chosen for the bottom layer of each flower was also used for the center of that flower.

PREPARATION

1. **From the dark blue background fabric, cut:**
   - Four strips, 2¼in x width of fabric (binding)

2. Use a white pencil or chalk pencil to mark a rectangle 37in x 42in on the remaining dark blue background fabric. This will be the size of your finished wallhanging. It is not cut to size at this stage as the dense stitching on this quilt sometimes distorts the fabric. It is better, therefore, to complete the appliqué before squaring up the background at a later stage.

3. Enlarge Templates A – D on a photocopier set to enlarge by 240%.

4. Trace the enlarged shapes on to the dull side of the freezer paper. Cut another five pieces of freezer paper a little larger than Templates A and B. Staple them together with the traced shape on top. Carefully cut around the traced shape through all the layers of freezer paper, to make six copies at once. Repeat to make 10 copies of Templates C and D. Given that it would be difficult to cut through 10 layers of paper, make them in two batches of five layers each.

APPLIQUÉ

1. Arrange these paper shapes on the background fabric, inside the lines drawn in step 2. Refer to the photograph of the quilt for guidance. When you are happy with your arrangement, number each shape – for example, Flower 2 upper layer and Flower 2 lower layer. Take a digital photograph if you have a camera. Lightly mark where shapes lie underneath others by tracing the upper shape on to the lower one. As you lift the paper shapes off the background fabric, cut these underlying shapes at least ¼in outside the traced lines (see Diagram 1).

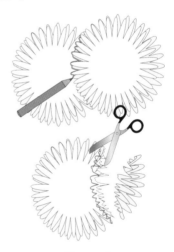

Diagram 1

2. Trace the complete and altered shapes on to the paper side of the fusible web. Include the broken lines and mark the top edge of the flower to make alignment of the layers easier when you fuse the fabric shapes. Write the number of each shape on the fusible web.

3. Use a compass to draw 10 circles with a radius of 1⅜in and six circles with a radius of 1½in on to the fusible web. These will be the flower centers for the small and large flowers respectively.

4. Trace shapes for individual petals for each of the small and large flowers on to the paper side of the fusible web. Several shapes are provided to give your flowers some variety. Each large flower will require 16 – 18 petals, so trace 100 in total. Each small flower will require 15 or 16 petals, so trace 155 in total.

5. Refer to the instructions for the Double-sided Fusible Web method on page 16 as you complete the next steps.

6. Cut the shapes out of the fusible web about ¼in outside the traced lines. Fuse them to the wrong side of your chosen fabrics. The individual petal shapes can be cut and fused in groups, which saves fiddling with small individual petals at this stage.

7. Cut out the circular center of each A, B, C and D shape. Do not cut in from the edge of the fabric, but use sharp embroidery scissors to make a slit close to the line, then cut accurately on the line. Use these fabric circles for the flower centers.

8. Peel the backing paper off all the fabric shapes. Lay them out on the background fabric, referring to your digital photo so that you can replicate your preferred design. Then fuse them in place. If you prefer, you might work in 'batches', fusing the shapes in groups and sewing them before fusing the next batch. This will reduce fraying.

9. Refer to the instructions for free motion stitching on page 23. Use a stabilizer behind your work – either a tear away stabilizer or freezer paper. Caroline worked her appliqué with three lines of stitching – two lines at this stage and then a third when quilting. If you prefer a less dense look for your stitching, free motion stitch twice around the bottom layer of each flower and only once around the middle layer and the individual petals. Then, when quilting, work a second line of stitching on the upper layer and individual petals – giving you two lines of stitching throughout. Caroline recommends completing the first line of stitching on every flower before returning to complete the second line. This will help keep the quilt top flat.

10. Work your free motion stitching in an even, moderate speed, slowing down a little around tight curves, such as at the tips of the petals. Try to avoid stopping and starting on a curve.

11. Pin a piece of tulle or netting behind each flower center before fusing it to the flower. It will act as a stabilizer as you work small continuous circles over the surface of the flower center; it remains in the quilt. Trim the tulle or netting right next to the edge of the flower center when this stitching is completed.

FINISH THE QUILT

1. Referring to Preparing the Quilt Top for Quilting in General Quiltmaking Instructions, page 94, layer the backing, batting and quilt ready for quilting. Pin baste.

2. Quilt as desired. *Delightful Dahlias* was machine quilted by Caroline. She stitched around all of the flowers with monofilament thread, and then worked another line of stitching using rayon machine embroidery threads around the middle layer of the flowers and the individual petals. Finally she quilted in a continuous circular pattern in the background, using a dark blue metallic thread.

3. Trim the background fabric to 42in x 37in (107cm x 94cm) with right angles at each corner.

4. Join the four strips cut for the binding end to end to make one long strip. Use it to bind the quilt, referring to Binding in General Quiltmaking Basics, page 94.

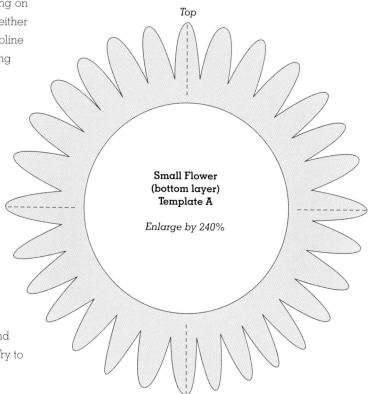

Top

Small Flower
(bottom layer)
Template A

Enlarge by 240%

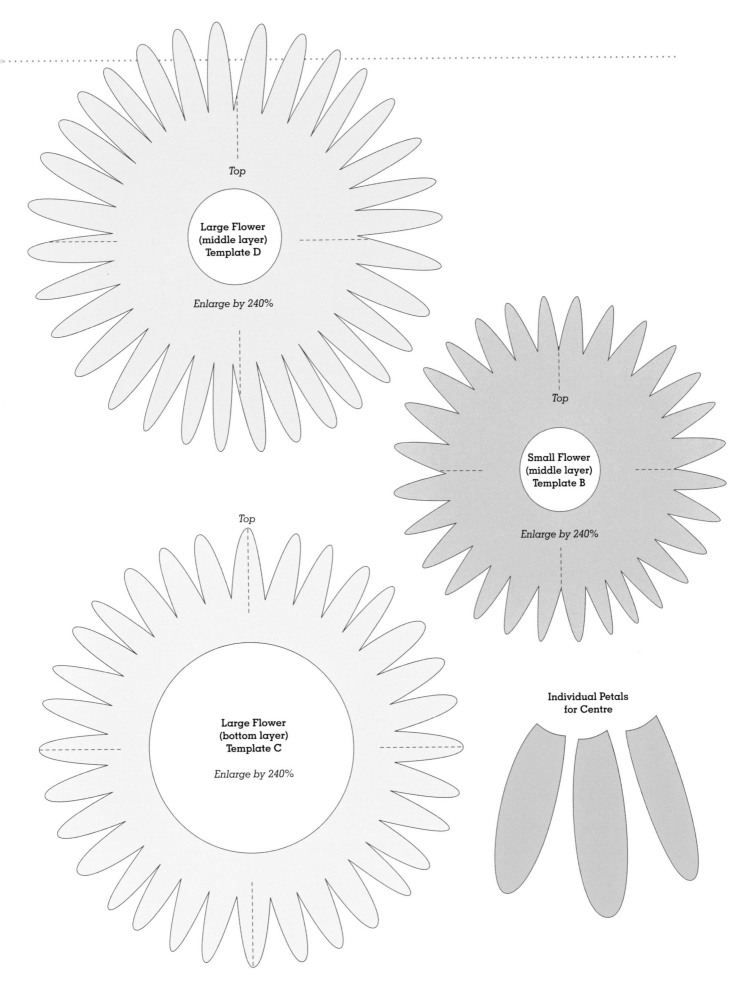

Top

**Large Flower
(middle layer)
Template D**

Enlarge by 240%

Top

**Small Flower
(middle layer)
Template B**

Enlarge by 240%

Top

**Large Flower
(bottom layer)
Template C**

Enlarge by 240%

**Individual Petals
for Centre**

Delightful Dahlias

Hidden Treasures

Finished size: 47½in x 41½in (121cm x 105cm)

Hidden Treasures

Bright colorful flowers always star in the garden, but occasionally you will stumble across some more subdued examples that can come as a complete surprise. The tones chosen for the flowers in this wallhanging celebrate these 'hidden treasures'.

This project also gives you an opportunity to try reverse machine appliqué. Even though the colors are planned, there is still a delightful surprise – a hidden treasure – when the top fabric is cut back to reveal the layer underneath!

> Method used: Reverse appliqué
>
> Stitch used: Grass (or satin) stitch; free motion stitching

MATERIALS:

- 1⅜yd (1.25m) leafy print batik (background)
- An assortment of hand dyed and mottled fabrics in a variety of colors (flowers). See note.
- ⅜yd (30cm) ochre mottled fabric (binding)
- 1½yd (1.3m) backing fabric
- Batting at least 52in x 46in (131cm x 115cm)
- Freezer paper
- Double-sided fusible web
- Iron-on tear away fabric stabilizer
- Machine embroidery threads to match the flower and background fabrics
- Monofilament thread
- Lightweight bobbin thread to match the background fabric
- Quilting thread

- Small curved scissors or duck bill appliqué scissors
- Rotary cutter, ruler and mat
- Sewing machine with open-toed appliqué foot, straight stitch foot and quilting foot
- General sewing supplies

Note: As a guide, you will need a 12in (30cm) square of fabric for each of the four large flowers; a 9in (23cm) square of fabric for each of the 14 medium flowers; and a 6½in (17cm) square of fabric for each of the six small flowers. In addition, you will need scraps for the flower centers. Caroline recommends choosing the background fabric first, then selecting colors that work well with it for the flowers.

PREPARATION:

1. Enlarge the small flower shape on page 61 by 132% to give you the size for the medium flower and by 168% to give you the size for the large flower.

2. Trace a small, medium and large flower shape on to the dull side of the freezer paper. As the freezer paper templates are re-usable, start with just one of each size. Make fresh ones as needed.

3. Trace four large flower centers, 14 medium flower centers, and six smaller flower centers on to fusible web, leaving about ½in between shapes. Cut the shapes out about ¼in outside the traced lines. Fuse them to the wrong side of the fabric you have chosen to use, then cut them out accurately on the line.

INITIAL APPLIQUÉ

1. The flowers in this wallhanging have been positioned in six groups. Flowers in one group don't overlap flowers in another group. The benefit of grouping the flowers in this way is that you can work on one group at a time and complete it before moving to the next group. This reduces fraying of your flower fabrics.

2. To add a flower to your wallhanging, lightly iron its freezer paper template to the right side of the background fabric in the position where you want the flower to be. Pin the square of appliqué fabric for the flower on the wrong side of the background fabric immediately behind the freezer paper. The right side of the flower fabric should be against the wrong side of the background fabric.

3. Using thread to match the background fabric, straight stitch around the edge of the freezer paper using a free motion method – this saves you from having to twist and turn the background fabric while you work.

4. Using curved embroidery scissors or duck bill appliqué scissors, trim away the background fabric ⅛in inside the stitching to reveal the fabric you've chosen for your flower beneath it. (You will trim back further later on.) Leave the entire square of flower fabric in place at this stage, but pin it out of the way so that you don't stitch over it when adding other flowers nearby.

5. Repeat steps 2 – 4 for other flowers in the group. Where flowers overlap, you will be cutting away some of the fabric for the underlying flower.

GRASS STITCH APPLIQUÉ

1. Peel the backing paper off the flower centers for each flower in the group and fuse them in place.

2. Trim the raw edges of the background fabric right next to the straight stitching around each flower. Position tear away stabilizer behind the flower you will be stitching.

3. Referring to the detailed instructions for grass stitch on page 22, grass stitch around each flower using a rayon thread to match the flower fabric in the top of the machine and a lightweight bobbin thread in the bobbin. The grass stitch may need to be mirrored on your machine, because you want the straight edge to be just on the flower fabric and the irregular side of the stitching overlapping on to the background fabric, covering the straight stitches you completed earlier. If your machine does not have grass stitch, you can use satin stitch instead.

4. After stitching right around the raw edges of the flower, gently remove the stabilizer from the back of your work. Support the stitching line as you do this to avoid distortion. Trim the excess flower fabric on the back of the quilt just outside the stitching you have just completed

5. Repeat steps 3 and 4 for each flower in the group.

6. Change to a quilting (or darning) foot. Place a fresh piece of stabilizer behind your work. Using thread to match the flower – the same thread used for the grass or satin stitching – work two lines of tiny loops around the flower center to hold it in place, working in free motion. Then work up to 10 large loops on each petal. Remove the stabilizer.

FINISH THE QUILT

1. Once you have completed the initial appliqué and grass stitching for an entire group of flowers, repeat the process for the remaining groups in turn.

2. Press your quilt top ready for quilting and binding. Referring to Preparing the Quilt Top for Quilting in General Quiltmaking Instructions, page 94, layer the backing, batting and quilt ready for quilting. Pin baste.

3. Quilt as desired. *Hidden Treasures* was machine quilted by Larraine Smith of Mudgee, Australia. She stitched around all of the flowers and then inside the line of grass stitching on the flower fabric using monofilament thread. Using a cotton thread, she then stitched loops and ferns on the background

4. Trim the background fabric to 47½in x 41½in (121cm x 105cm) with right angles at each corner.

5. From the mottled mustard fabric, cut five strips, 2¼in x width of fabric. Join them end to end to make one long strip. Use it to bind the quilt, referring to Binding in General Quiltmaking Instructions on page 94.

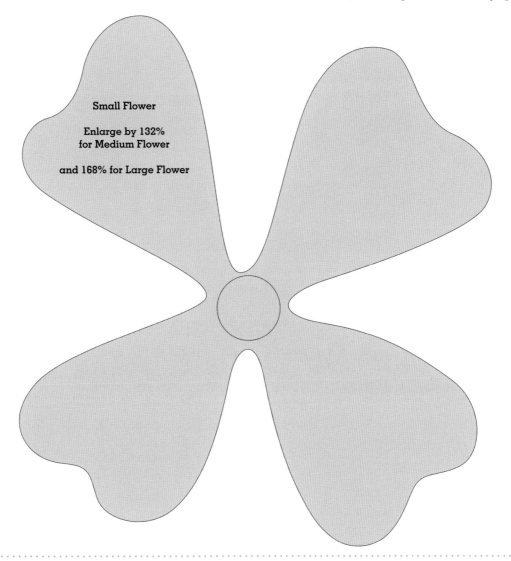

Small Flower

Enlarge by 132% for Medium Flower

and 168% for Large Flower

Sun & Surf

Finished size: 72in x 80in (183cm x 204cm)

Finished block size: 8in

Love to Machine Appliqué

Sun & Surf

This bright quilt is built on the traditional pieced block
Snail's Trail, which has always looked like surf waves
to Caroline, and reminded her of long, lazy days at the beach.
Coupled with it are a sand-colored background fabric, a variety of
beach themed appliqué motifs and quilting designs that
mimic water and water creatures.
This one is for beach lovers everywhere.

> Method used: Double-sided fusible web
>
> Stitch used: Blanket stitch

MATERIALS:

- 2¼yd (2.1m) mottled sand fabric (center appliqué background and Border 2)
- 2¼yd (2.1m) green/blue print fabric (Snail's Trail blocks and appliqué)
- 2⅛yd (2m) mottled light aqua fabric (Snail's Trail blocks)
- ⅜yd (30cm) mottled light blue fabric (Border 3 corners)
- An assortment of print fabrics (center appliqué)
- ¼yd (15cm) each of five lemon, orange or tan tone-on-tone fabrics (Border 3 appliqué)
- ⅝yd (55cm) green mottled fabric (binding)
- 4¾yd (4.3m) backing fabric
- Batting at least 76in x 84in (193cm x 214cm)
- Easy Angle ruler (optional)
- Double-sided fusible web
- Freezer paper (optional)
- Teflon coated appliqué mat

- Compass
- Machine embroidery threads (appliqué)
- Monofilament thread (quilting)
- Blue machine embroidery thread (quilting)
- Rotary cutter, ruler and mat
- Sewing machine with open-toed appliqué foot and ¼in foot
- General sewing supplies

Note: *If you are using an Easy Angle ruler, refer to the instructions at the end of the Cutting section.*

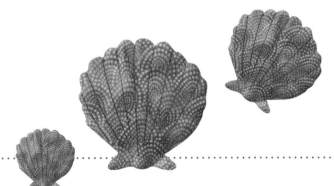

CUTTING:

From the mottled sand fabric, cut:
- One 25½in x 33½in rectangle (center background)
- Six strips, 8½in x width of fabric (Border 2)

From the green/blue print fabric, cut:
- Five strips, 1⅞in x width of fabric (Snail's Trail blocks)
- 11 strips, 2½in x width of fabric (Snail's Trail blocks). Crosscut these strips to yield 96 rectangles, 2½in x 4½in (A).
- 11 strips, 2⅞in. Crosscut these strips to yield 144 squares, 2⅞in, then cut each square once on the diagonal to yield 288 half-square triangles (B).*

From the mottled light aqua fabric, cut:
- Five strips, 1⅞in x width of fabric (Snail's Trail blocks)
- 11 strips, 2½in x width of fabric (Snail's Trail blocks). Crosscut these strips to yield 96 rectangles, 2½in x 4½in (C).
- 11 strips, 2⅞in. Crosscut these strips to yield 144 squares, 2⅞in, then cut each square once on the diagonal to yield 288 half-square triangles (D).*

From the mottled light blue fabric, cut:
- Four squares, 8½in (Border 3 corners)

From the green mottled fabric, cut:
- Eight strips, 2¼in x width of fabric (binding)

If you are using an Easy Angle ruler to cut the B and D triangles, cut strips 2½in wide and from them crosscut with the Easy Angle ruler to yield 288 B triangles and 288 D triangles.

Tip: To avoid cutting and sewing small shapes for appliqué, look for opportunities to 'cheat'. It's often possible to cut a larger shape and then add stitching to create the illusion of a series of separate pieces. For example, trace the shape for the base of the two flip flops as one piece; add the strips on top; and then blanket stitch around the entire upper flip flop so that it appears to have been made from a piece of fabric that is quite separate from the lower flip flop.

Tip: When adding layers of smaller shapes to a base appliqué shape, cut them a little larger than required along those edges that sit on the outside of the shape underneath. The light blue pattern on the middle surfboard, for example, can be cut slightly outside the traced lines. Peel the backing paper off the shapes and press them lightly in place on top of the surfboard. The outer edges can then be cut back so that they are a precise match with the edge of the surfboard – thus achieving perfect placement with ease.

APPLIQUÉ THE QUILT CENTER:

1. Trace all the center appliqué patterns from pages 68 – 71 on to the paper side of the fusible web. Trace the small surfboard twice. Cut them out about ¼in outside the traced lines. Use a compass to draw a circle with a radius of 1⅞in for the larger beach ball.

2. Refer to the instructions for the Double-sided Fusible Web method on page 16 as you work on the following steps.

3. Fuse the traced appliqué shapes to your chosen fabrics, then cut them out on the traced lines. Remove the backing paper and place the shapes on the large rectangle of mottled sand fabric cut for the center of the quilt – keep in mind that the background will be trimmed, so your shapes should be at least 1½in from the raw edges. When you are happy with their arrangement, fuse, then blanket stitch in place using matching machine embroidery threads. Refer to the instructions for blanket stitch on page 22.

4. Trim the sand rectangle to 24½in x 32½in.

MAKE THE SNAIL'S TRAIL BLOCKS

Snail's Trail block – make 48

1. Sew a 1⅞in strip of green/blue print fabric to a 1⅞in strip of mottled light aqua fabric. Press the seam towards the green/blue print fabric. Crosscut this strip set to yield 22 segments, 1⅞in (see Diagram 1).

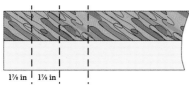

1⅞ in   1⅞ in

Diagram 1

2. Join a pair of segments together with the green/blue print squares diagonally opposite each other to make a Four-patch unit (see diagram). Repeat with all the segments to yield a total of 11 Four-patch units.

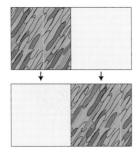

Four-patch unit – make 48

3. Repeat steps 1 and 2 with the remaining strips of green/blue and mottled light aqua fabrics, to make a total of 48 Four-patch units.

4. Lay a Four-patch unit on your work surface with a green/blue square in the upper left corner. Sew a mottled light aqua D triangle to its top and bottom edges (see Diagram 2). Press seams towards the D triangles. Repeat for all the Four-patch units.

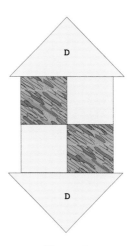

Diagram 2

5. Now sew a green/blue B triangle to the left and right edges of each Four-patch unit (see Diagram 3). Again, press seams towards the triangles. Trim the little 'ears' of fabric from each block.

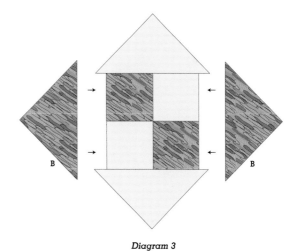

Diagram 3

6. Stitch each remaining B triangle to a D triangle, to yield a total of 192 pieced squares.

7. Referring to Diagram 4, stitch one of these squares to the right end of the A and C rectangles. Take care with the fabric placement: when sewing a square to the A rectangles, the green/blue triangle should be sewn to the end of the rectangle; when sewing a square to the C rectangles, the light aqua triangle should be sewn to the end of the rectangle. Press seams towards the rectangles.

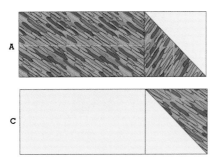

Diagram 4

8. Lay out two green/blue rectangles and two light aqua rectangles around the center units, referring to the Block Layout Diagram. Take care that each unit is orientated exactly as shown in the diagram, otherwise the overall pattern of the block won't work.

Block Layout Diagram

9. Begin assembling the Snail's Trail block by sewing the green/blue rectangle to the center unit with a partial seam. That is, only sew about two thirds of the way along the top edge of the center seam (see Diagram 5). Press the seam towards the rectangle.

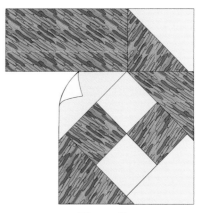

Diagram 5

10. Sew a light aqua rectangle to the right edge of the center unit+green/blue rectangle. Follow this by sewing a green/blue rectangle to the bottom edge, and then another light aqua rectangle to the left edge. Finally, go back to the partial seam and complete it, stitching the first green/blue rectangle across the top of the block (see Diagram 6). Press the block.

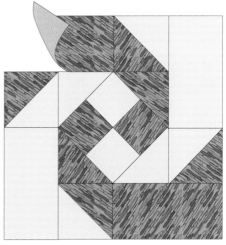

Diagram 6

11. Repeat steps 8 – 10 to make 48 Snail's Trail blocks. They should measure 8½in from raw edge to raw edge.

ADD BORDER 1

1. Lay out eight Snail's Trail blocks in two rows of four. Each block should be orientated exactly the same way. Sew the blocks in each of these rows together, then sew the rows to the left and right edges of the quilt. Press seams towards the quilt center.

2. Lay out 10 Snail's Trail blocks in two rows of five. Each block should be orientated in exactly the same way, so that when these borders are added to the quilt, they match the orientation of the blocks in the side borders. Refer to the photo of the quilt for guidance. Sew the blocks in each of these rows together, then sew the rows to the top and bottom edges of the quilt. Press seams towards the quilt center. Your quilt should now measure 40½in x 48½in.

ADD BORDER 2

1. Trace all the shell appliqué patterns from pages 68 – 71 on to the paper side of fusible web. Also trace the inner dashed pencil lines: when the fabric is fused to the background fabric, these lines can be lightly transferred on to the fabric using a light box or by holding the appliqué shape against a window. Trace each of the shell shapes five times, then choose one to trace one more time to make a total of 26 shells.

2. Cut all the shapes out about ¼in outside the traced lines. Fuse them to the wrong side of your chosen fabrics, then cut them out on the traced lines.

3. Stitch the inner lines before peeling the backing paper off the fusible web. Caroline used free motion stitching worked with threads somewhat darker than the appliqué fabrics

> **Tip:** When stitching the inner lines on the shell shapes, place a piece of freezer paper behind the work to act as a stabilizer. It is easy to tear off afterwards if you use a short stitch length.

4. Join the six strips of mottled sand fabric cut for Border 2 end to end using diagonal seams, referring to Borders in General Quiltmaking Basics on page 94.

5. From this long strip, cut two strips 48½in and two strips 56½in. Lightly mark each border strip ¼in from each end, and then every 8in along its length (see Diagram 7). Finger press the fabric at these marks.

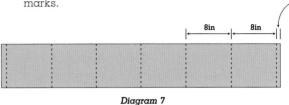

Diagram 7

6. Using the quilt photo as a guide, center a shell in each segment created by the creases. Take into account which strip you will be sewing to which edge of the quilt so that you can distribute the different shapes around the quilt, and orientate them so that they will all be facing in the right direction once they're joined to the quilt. Blanket stitch them in place.

7. Stitch the two shorter appliquéd borders to the left and right edges of the quilt. Then stitch the longer strips to the top and bottom edges of the quilt. Press seams towards the center of the quilt.

ADD BORDER 3

1. Trace the dolphin shape from page 71 twice on to the paper side of fusible web. Trace it again on to a sheet of paper, then turn the paper over and trace it through on to the other side. This will give you a reversed dolphin shape. Trace the reversed dolphin twice on to the paper side of fusible web.

2. Cut the dolphins out about ¼in outside the traced lines. Fuse them to the wrong side of your chosen fabrics, then cut them out on the traced lines. Sufficient fabric has been included in the Materials list to enable you to use the green/blue print fabric for the dolphins, as Caroline has done, if you wish.

3. Center each dolphin on a light aqua square cut for the Border 3 corners. Stitch in place using blanket stitch.

4. Use the remaining 30 Snail's Trail blocks to create

two rows of eight blocks each for the left and right edges of the quilt as you did for Border 1. Stitch these borders to the quilt.

5. For the top and bottom borders, join seven blocks together. Then join an appliquéd dolphin block to each end of these rows, orientating them so that the dolphins face towards the center of the strip. Stitch these rows to the quilt.

QUILTING AND BINDING

1. Press your quilt top ready for quilting and binding. Cut the length of backing fabric in half. Remove the selvages and join the two lengths down a long edge.

2. Referring to Preparing the Quilt Top for Quilting in General Quiltmaking Instructions, page 94, layer the backing, batting and quilt ready for quilting. Pin baste.

3. Caroline quilted *Sun & Surf* in the ditch around all the appliqué shapes and in the seam lines joining the borders to the quilt. She used a monofilament thread in the top of the machine. She then stitched in a meandering pattern with cream thread on the sand background. The Snail's Trail blocks have fish and dolphins quilted on them using the patterns from page 71.

4. Join the eight strips cut for the binding end to end to make one long strip. Use it to bind the quilt, referring to Binding in General Quiltmaking Instructions, page 94.

under

under

Love to Machine Appliqué

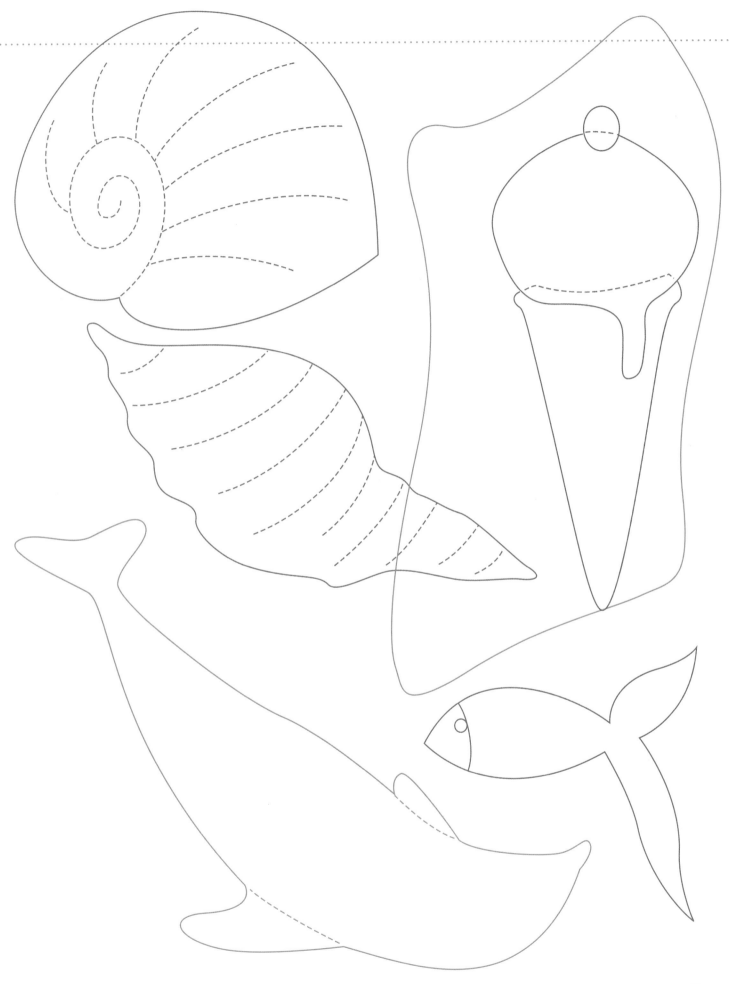

Sun & Surf

Summer Nights

Finished size: 35½in x 41½in (90cm x 105cm)

Love to Machine Appliqué

Summer Nights

A heavily quilted black tone-on-tone print background
on this dramatic wallhanging enhances
the effect of the three dimensional appliqué.
Use a variety of subtley different shades of fabric or even
hand dyed fabrics for the gladioli and lilies to make them remarkably
true-to-life. Just be warned – your guests won't be able
to stop themselves from reaching out to touch them.

> Method used: Freezer paper with or without glue; 3D appliqué; bias tape appliqué
>
> Stitch used: Blind hem stitch

MATERIALS:

- 1⅛yd (1m) black tone-on-tone print fabric (background)
- ⅛yd (10cm) each of three or four yellow tone-on-tone print fabrics (gladioli)
- ½yd (35cm) green tone-on-tone fabric #1 (gladioli leaves and stems)
- ⅜yd (30cm) green tone-on-tone fabric #2 (gladioli leaf and stem)
- Fat eighths of four orange tone-on-tone print fabrics (lily flowers and buds). Caroline recommends two light and two darker tones.
- Fat eighth of dark green tone-on-tone print fabric (lily leaves and stems)
- ¼yd (15cm) dark pink tone-on-tone print fabric (geranium flowers)
- ¼yd (15cm) red tone-on-tone print fabric (geranium flowers)
- Fat eighths of two lime green tone-on-tone print fabrics (geranium leaves and stems)
- ⅜yd (25cm) striped fabric (binding). See note.
- 12in (30cm) square of green tulle or netting (geranium leaves)
- 1⅜yd (1.3m) backing fabric

- Batting at least 40in x 46in (100cm x 115cm)
- High loft batting at least 10in x 15in (25cm x 38cm) (trapunto for geranium flowers)
- ½in and ¼in bias makers
- ⅛in bias press bar
- Draftsmen's tracing paper or a plastic page protector (from stationery store) and Chinagraph or other pencil designed to write on plastic
- Glue stick suitable for use on fabric
- Double-sided fusible web
- Template plastic and permanent marking pen
- Iron-on tear away fabric stabilizer
- Water-soluble fabric stabilizer
- Freezer paper
- Spray starch
- Rayon machine embroidery threads in shades suitable for embellishing the appliqué
- Monofilament thread (quilting)
- Jeans 70/10 needle and 60/8 and 90/14 needles
- Rotary cutter, ruler and mat
- Sewing machine and machine embroidery hoop
- General sewing supplies

NOTE: *Caroline cut her binding on the bias so that the stripes printed on the fabric were on the diagonal. If you wish to achieve a similar look, you will need to purchase ¾yd (70cm) of striped fabric.*

PREPARATION

1. Trim the selvages from the black tone-on-tone print fabric. Then use spray starch in keeping with the manufacturer's instructions to starch the fabric. This will give added body to the quilt top before you begin to appliqué.

PREPARE THE GLADIOLI

1. Cut a strip of freezer paper 8in (20cm) wide and 37½in (95cm) long. Referring to Diagram 1 as a guide, draw three long leaves on its dull side. Number them as shown in the diagram. When you are satisfied with the shapes you have drawn, cut them out on the lines.

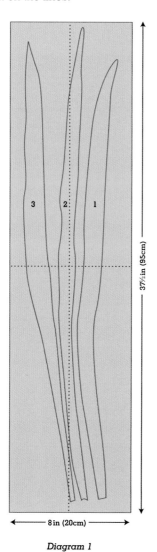

Diagram 1

2. Use either the Freezer Paper with Glue or Without Glue method to stitch these leaves. Caroline chose to prepare her shapes with glue because of the tight curves at the top of each leaf, but adapt the following instructions if you prefer to work without glue. Iron the shape for leaves 1 and 3 on to the wrong side of green tone-on-tone print fabric #1, leaving at least ½in between them. Cut each shape out a scant ¼in outside the paper template.

3. Following the directions provided for Freezer Paper with Glue on page 12, fold the seam allowances over on to the freezer paper and glue them in place, ready for appliquéing.

4. From the remaining green tone-on-tone print fabric #1, cut sufficient bias strips 1in wide so that when joined end to end the strip will be about 60in (150cm) long.

5. Repeat steps 2 and 3 to prepare leaf 2 from green tone-on-tone fabric #2. Then cut sufficient bias strips ½in wide from this fabric so that when joined end to end the strip will be about 28in (70cm) long.

6. Trace the shapes for both the small and large gladioli flowers and the two calyxes from page 80 on to template plastic using the permanent marking pen. (Do not trace the shapes for the 3D petals at this stage.) Cut them out accurately. Mark the front of each template.

7. Use these templates to trace one of each shape for the large flower, seven of each shape for the small flower, five calyx #1, seven calyx #1 reversed and three calyx #2 on to the dull side of the freezer paper.

8. Trace one of each of the shapes for the 3D petals and two of the buds for calyx #2 from page 80 on to the freezer paper.

PREPARE THE LILIES

1. Trace lily shapes 1 – 3 and the bud shape from page 81 on to template plastic using the permanent marking pen. (Do not trace the shapes for the 3D petals at this stage.) Cut them out accurately. Mark the front of each template.

2. Use templates 1 – 3 to trace three of each shape on to the dull side of the freezer paper. Note that the broken lines on these patterns indicate where edges will sit under other shapes, and don't need to be turned under. Then trace the bud five times on to the freezer paper.

3. Trace shapes 4 and 5 for the 3D petals and leaves #1 and #2 from page 81 on to freezer paper.

4. From the fat eighth of dark green tone-on-tone print fabric, cut sufficient bias strips 1in wide so that when joined end to end the strip will be about 60in (150cm) long.

5. Enlarge the lily placement guide on page 81 by 200% and trace it on to the plastic page protector using a Chinagraph pencil..

PREPARE THE GERANIUMS

1. Trace the two leaf shapes, flower base and flower petals for the geraniums from page 79 on to template plastic using the permanent marking pen. Cut them out accurately. Mark the front of each template.

2. Use these templates to trace three leaf #1, two leaf #1 reversed, one leaf #2, two leaf #2 reversed and five flower bases on to the dull side of the freezer paper. You might find it useful to trace one or two extra leaves so that you have more options when you come to arrange them on your quilt.

3. From each of the fat eighths of lime green tone-on-tone print fabric, cut sufficient bias strips ⅞in wide so if they were joined end to end the strip would be about 30in (75cm) long.

STITCH THE GLADIOLI

1. Pin the gladioli leaves to the background fabric, referring to the photograph and Diagram 2 as a guide. Stitch them in place using blind hem stitch. See page 19 for details.

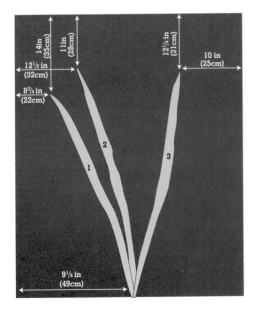

Diagram 2

2. Cut the background fabric from behind the leaves and remove the freezer paper.

3. Join the bias strips cut from green tone-on-tone fabric #1 end to end to make one long strip. Press the seams open and trim them so that they are even with the edges of the strip. Use a ½in bias maker or your preferred method to turn under the edges of this strip ready for appliqué.

4. Repeat step 3 with the bias strips cut from green tone-on-tone fabric #2. Use the ¼in bias maker with these strips.

5. Referring to the photograph for guidance, pin the stems to the background and appliqué them in place using blind hem stitch.

6. Using the Freezer Paper with Glue method, following the instructions on page 12, make the two dimensional petals for the gladioli flowers. The broken lines on the left and right petals indicate where the seam allowance sits under the center petal and does not need to be glued under. Pin the petals for all the flowers in place. Caroline used one large and four small flowers on the left stem in her quilt, and three small flowers on the right stem. Blind hem stitch all of these petals in place, except the center petals for the top flower on each stem.

7. Fuse two of the freezer paper shapes for calyx #1, four calyx #1 reversed and two calyx #2 to the wrong side of green tone-on-tone fabric #1. Cut the shapes out a scant ¼in outside the paper templates. Glue the seam allowance over the freezer paper.

8. Repeat step 7 with all the remaining calyx shapes and green tone-on-tone print fabric #2 and then with the two calyx #2 buds on the appropriate yellow fabrics.

9. At the top of each stem, position a calyx under the top-most flower. Then tuck the remaining calyxes underneath each other, working up towards the top edge of the quilt. When you have an arrangement that you like, pin the calyxes in place. Then tuck the small calyx #2 buds under the top calyx on each stem and pin.

10. Stitch all the calyxes and the two calyx #2 buds in place using blind hem stitch. The stitching on the lower edge of the calyxes that will have the 3D buds tucked under them will need to be unpicked later on. For this reason, it is best to increase the

Tip: - Instead of cutting notches all around the seam allowances, use pinking shears to cut around the three dimensional shapes. (Take care not to cut into the sewn seam.) All the 'notches' made by the shears will help you achieve smooth edges once you turn the three dimensional shapes right side out.

yellow fabric, following the directions for the second method in 3D Appliqué on page 28.

14. After turning the petals right side out, press them carefully. Fold each petal in half and stitch a small tuck, starting about ½in from the lower edge and stitching for ¾in (see Diagram 3). Although this tiny tuck should be no more than ⅛in wide, it does help make these petals more realistic.

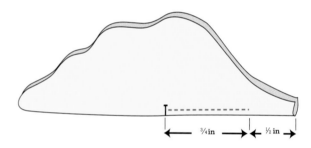

¾in   ½in

Diagram 3

length of your stitches along these edges so that the unpicking is easier. (The 3D buds are not sewn at this stage because the background fabric and the freezer paper underneath the calyxes needs to be removed first.)

11. Cut away the background fabric and remove all the freezer paper behind the shapes you have now sewn. Stitch the center petals on the top-most flower on each stem. Then cut away any excess stems from behind the flowers.

12. Position tear away stabilizer behind each of the center petals and stitch stamens using machine embroidery thread. Caroline worked the stamens on her quilt in a very narrow satin stitch with a single scallop pattern on the top of each stamen. Hand embroidery is another option. Carefully remove the stabilizer.

13. Make the 3D petals from 3in x 3¼in rectangles of

15. Butt the bases of a left and right three dimensional petal together and zigzag stitch for about ½in (see Diagram 4).

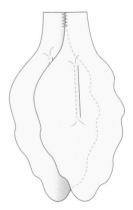

Diagram 4

16. Place the center petal on your work surface, right side down. Center the joined left and right petals on top of it, then stitch all three petals together with a zigzag stitch.

17. Repeat steps 15 and 16 with all the sets of three dimensional petals. Set them aside to attach later.

STITCH THE LILIES

1. Referring to the photograph for guidance, pin the lily buds and stems in place on the background fabric, curving the stems as you work. When you are happy with the arrangement, stitch them in place using blind hem stitch.

2. Make the buds and petals 1 – 3 for each flower using the Freezer Paper with Glue method. Use slightly different shades for the petals to add interest. Position them on the background fabric using the plastic or tracing paper placement guide. Then stitch them in place using blind hem stitch.

3. Remove the backing fabric and freezer paper from behind these shapes. Position tear away stabilizer behind each of the buds and flowers. Work lines of triple straight stitching in machine embroidery thread on the buds and stitch stamens on the flowers using the same stitch, with a single scallop at the end.

4. Make 3D petals #4 and #5 and two leaf 1 and three leaf 2 following the directions for the second method in 3D Appliqué on page 28.

5. Use the placement guide to help you position the petals and see where they fold over and are not stitched. The lower edge of petal #4 sits under the lower edge of petal #5. You will need to tuck the end of petal #4 out of the way so that when the two petals are joined, they make a smooth curve at the base of the flower. Stitch these petals in place.

6. Turn the leaves right side out and press. Place them on firm tear away stabilizer and stitch the veins using triple straight stitch and machine embroidery thread. Remove the stabilizer.

7. Unpick a little of the stitching on the stems and tuck the ends of the leaves under them. Re-stitch the stems, catching the leaf ends.

STITCHING THE GERANIUMS

1. Make the geranium leaves from two different lime green fabrics using the Freezer Paper with Glue method. Similarly, make three red and two dark pink flower bases. Pin them on the background fabric, referring to the photograph for guidance. If you have a digital camera, take a photograph of your arrangement. This will allow you to remove the leaves and flower bases to stitch the stems.

2. To make the thin stems for the geranium leaves and flowers, use the ⅞in bias strips. Fold them in half, wrong sides together. Stitch the long edges together using a ¼in seam to make a tube, then trim the seam allowance. Insert the rounded end of a ⅛in quilter's press bar into the tube. Roll the seam allowance to the center of the flat side of the press bar. Press the seam open, slipping the bar through the tube as you go.

3. Position the stems on the background, then remove the flowers and leaves. Stitch the stems in place using blind hem stitch. Re-arrange the flowers and leaves at the top of each stem, and blind hem stitch them.

4. Remove the background fabric and freezer paper from behind the flower bases and any leaves that aren't overlapping others.

5. Cut pieces of high loft batting a little larger than

each of the flower bases. Pin a piece behind each flower base. Working from the front of the quilt, stitch in the ditch around the edge of the flower base using a small free motion straight stitch with monofilament thread. Trim away the excess batting as close to the line of stitching as possible.

6. Cut a 4in x 10in rectangle from each of the dark pink fabric and the fusible web. Fuse the web to the wrong side of the fabric, then remove the backing paper. Fold the fabric in half, wrong sides together, and press to fuse the two layers together. Lightly trace eight petal #1 and four petal #2 on one side of the fabric, leaving ¼in between shapes.

7. Cut a piece of water-soluble stabilizer large enough to fit into your hoop. Pin the fused dark pink fabric on top, traced side uppermost. Use free motion straight stitching and machine embroidery thread to match the fabric, stitch just inside the edge of each petal. Work around each petal three times. Using black thread, stitch the center detail on each petal.

8. When all the petals have been stitched, remove the work from the hoop and rinse the water-soluble stabilizer away. Cut out each petal just outside the stitching.

9. Repeat steps 5 – 8 with a 12in square of red fabric to make 12 Petal 1 and six Petal 2.

10. On a 12in square of water-soluble stabilizer, trace around the geranium leaf template three times with a permanent marking pen. Lay a 12in square of tulle on top of the stabilizer and secure both layers in your hoop. Straight stitch twice around the outer edge of the leaves using free motion stitching.

2. Follow the instructions for making tulle leaves in *Autumn Leaves* on page 51 to make three leaves. They will be attached to the quilt after it is quilted.

FINISH THE QUILT

1. Referring to Preparing the Quilt Top for Quilting in General Quiltmaking Instructions, page 94, layer the backing, batting and quilt ready for quilting. Pin baste.

2. Quilt as desired. *Summer Nights* was machine quilted by Caroline. She stitched around all of the appliquéd shapes with monofilament thread. She then worked the details on the gladioli and geranium leaves using rayon machine embroidery threads. The background was quilted in a dark cotton thread in free motion teardrop patterns. Quilting the background heavily will help make the appliqué stand out.

3. Square up the background fabric to 35½in x 41½in (90cm x 105cm) with right angles at each corner.

4. Join the strips cut for the binding end to end to make one long strip. Use it to bind the quilt, referring to Binding in General Quiltmaking Instructions on page 94.

5. Use the placement guide for the lily to pin the tips of the three dimensional petals in place. Blind stitch

them to the background fabric using monofilament thread, working only just enough stitches to hold them.

6. Position each set of 3D gladioli petals across the lower edge of the center flower petal with the center 3D petal face down (see Diagram 5). Stitch.

7. Turn the 3D flowers over and stitch their tips to the background fabric. Stitch the tips of the lily leaves in a similar manner.

8. Use a 90/14 needle and monofilament thread to work a few stitches in the center of each geranium flower to attach them to the flower bases.

9. Attach the 3D geranium leaves to the quilt with a row of stitching along their top edges using thread to match the stitching.

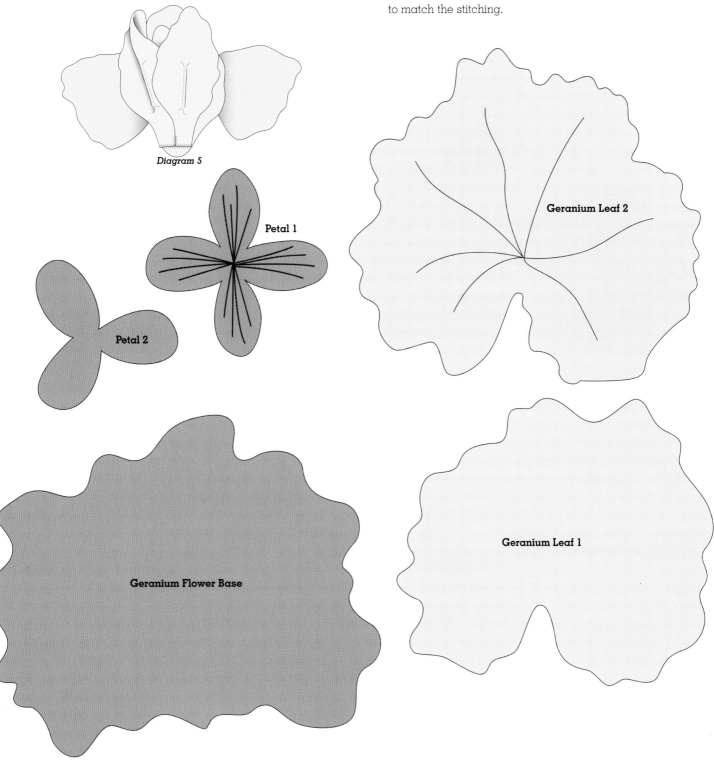

Diagram 5

Petal 1

Petal 2

Geranium Leaf 2

Geranium Leaf 1

Geranium Flower Base

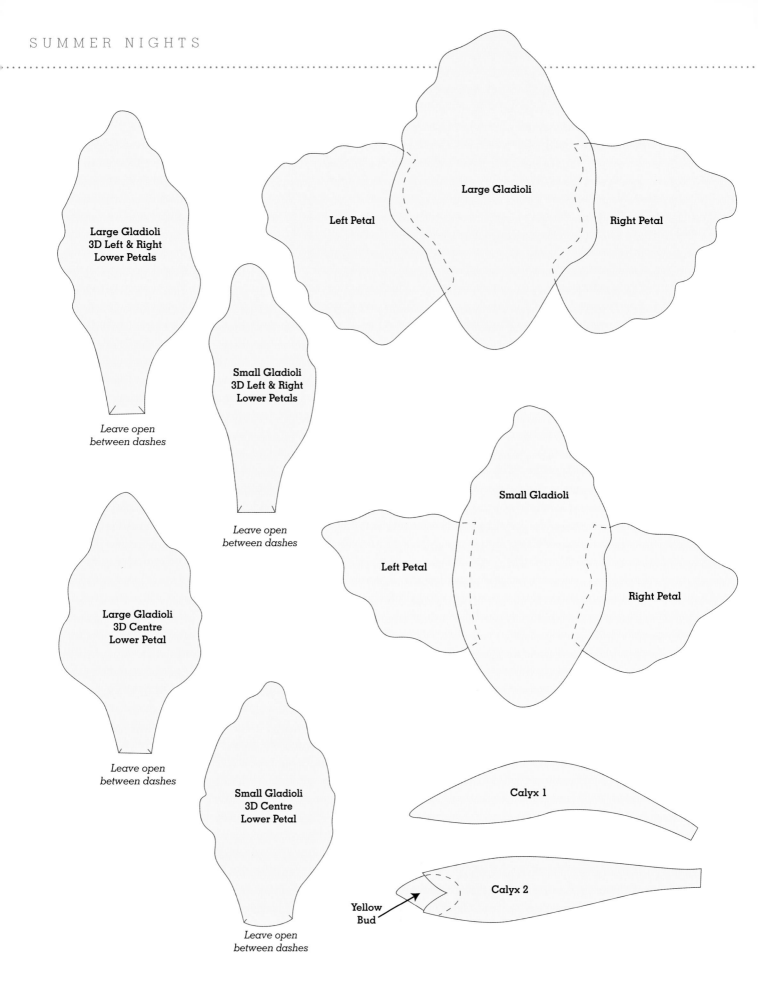

**Large Gladioli
3D Left & Right
Lower Petals**

*Leave open
between dashes*

**Small Gladioli
3D Left & Right
Lower Petals**

*Leave open
between dashes*

Left Petal

Large Gladioli

Right Petal

**Large Gladioli
3D Centre
Lower Petal**

*Leave open
between dashes*

Small Gladioli

Left Petal

Right Petal

**Small Gladioli
3D Centre
Lower Petal**

*Leave open
between dashes*

Calyx 1

Calyx 2

Yellow
Bud

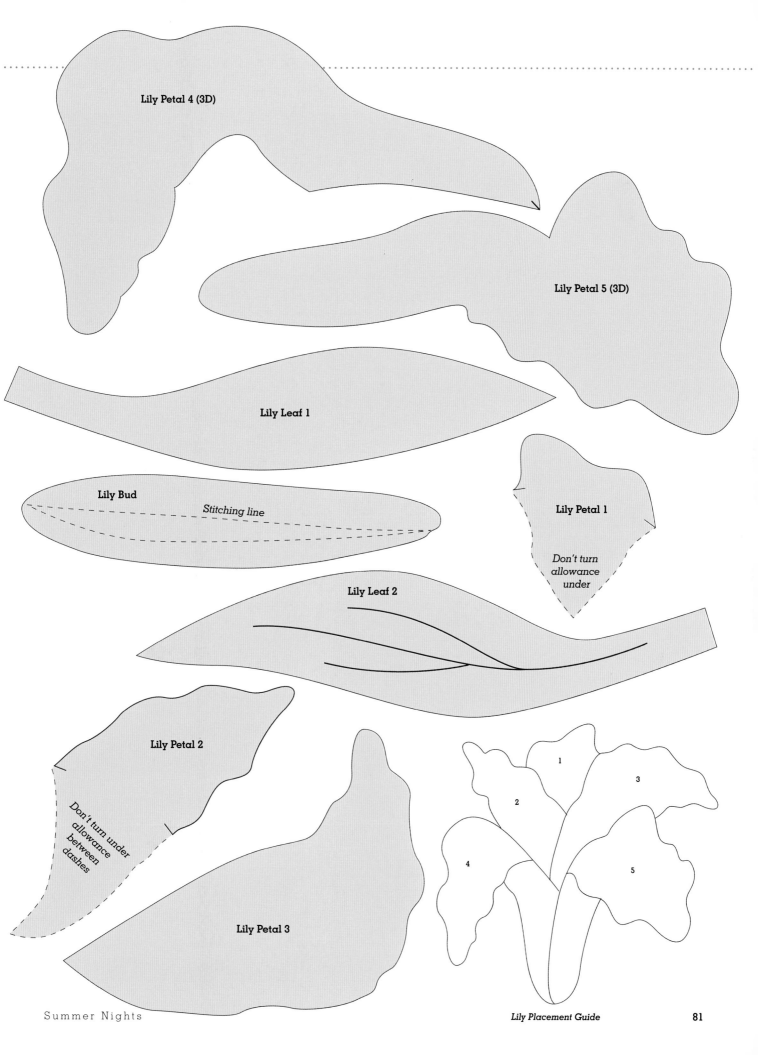

Lily Petal 4 (3D)

Lily Petal 5 (3D)

Lily Leaf 1

Lily Bud

Stitching line

Lily Petal 1

Don't turn
allowance
under

Lily Leaf 2

Lily Petal 2

Don't turn under
allowance
between
dashes

Lily Petal 3

1

2

3

4

5

Some Like it Hot

Finished size: 84in (213cm) square

Some Like it Hot

A collection of **black** and **white** print fabrics
inspired this **contemporary medallion** quilt.
When used with a hot pink hand dyed **background fabric**
and **just a touch** of lime green, the result is **striking** indeed.

Methods used: Double-sided fusible web;
bias tape appliqué

Stitches used: blind hem stitch; blanket stitch

MATERIALS:

- 5yd (4.5m) hot pink hand dyed fabric
  (background)
- An assortment of black and white print fabrics
  (appliqué). Caroline recommends that the
  fabrics span the value spectrum, from white
  prints on black backgrounds through to black
  prints on white backgrounds. Also choose
  prints that have a variety of different scales.
- ⅛yd (10cm) lime green fabric (appliqué)
- 1¾yd (1.5m) black and white stripe fabric (bias
  strips and binding). This is the amount needed
  for use with a bias tape maker, where the strips
  need to be cut twice as wide as they finish.
  If you are making bias strips using a different
  method, you may need to adjust the amount of
  fabric you buy.
- ¼yd (25cm) black and white polka dot print
  fabric #1 (Border 1)
- ½yd (40cm) black and white polka dot print
  fabric #2 (Border 3)

- 6yd (5m) backing fabric
- Batting at least 88in (225cm) square
- Template plastic and permanent marking pen
- Freezer paper
- Double-sided fusible web
- Pencil and fabric eraser or tailor's chalk or a dry,
  thin wedge of soap
- ¼in and ½in bias makers
- Spray starch
- Black cotton or rayon thread (blanket stitching)
- Monofilament thread (appliqué and quilting)
- Rotary cutter, ruler and mat
- Sewing machine with open toed appliqué foot
- General sewing supplies

CUTTING:

From the hot pink hand dyed fabric, cut:

- One square, 40in (quilt center)
- 12 strips, 10½in x width of fabric (Borders 2 and 4)

From the black and white striped fabric, cut:

- Nine strips, 2¼in x width of fabric (binding)
- lengths of ½in bias strips to total at least 100in long (stems on center heart). If you are not using a ¼in bias maker, cut your bias strips the appropriate width to make strips that will finish ¼in wide when appliquéd to the quilt.
- lengths of ½in bias strips to total at least 700in long (Border 4 vine). If you are not using a ¼in bias maker, cut your bias strips the appropriate width to make strips that will finish ¼in wide when appliquéd to the quilt.
- lengths of 1in bias strips to total at least 60in long (center heart). If you are not using a ½in bias maker, cut your bias strips the appropriate width to make strips that will finish ½in wide when appliquéd to the quilt.

From black and white polka dot print fabric #1, cut:

- Four strips, 2in x width of fabric (Border 1)

From black and white polka dot print fabric #2, cut:

- Seven strips, 2in x width of fabric (Border 3)

PREPARING TO APPLIQUÉ

1. Make templates from template plastic for the small (A) and large (B) leaves, the flower and the flower center, using the designs on page 88. Mark the front of each template.

2. Trace the shape for the curves in Borders 2 and 4 from page 88 on to freezer paper. Cut them out carefully.

3. Enlarge each of the four sections of the center heart shape and the shapes for the Border 2 and Border 4 Corner Guides on a photocopier set to enlarge by 240%. Join the sections of the heart shape together on the broken lines to create a complete heart. Trace it and the corner guides on to freezer paper.

Tip: - When making templates, work carefully so that they will have smooth edges. This will result, in turn, in smooth edges on your appliqué. If necessary, you can file the edges of your templates with very fine sandpaper to smooth them.

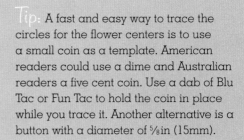

Tip: A fast and easy way to trace the circles for the flower centers is to use a small coin as a template. American readers could use a dime and Australian readers a five cent coin. Use a dab of Blu Tac or Fun Tac to hold the coin in place while you trace it. Another alternative is a button with a diameter of ⅝in (15mm).

4. Fold the 40in square of hot pink hand dyed fabric in half in each direction and press lightly to crease. Unfold the fabric. Fuse the freezer paper template for the large heart in the center of this square and trace around it lightly on the fabric. Remove the freezer paper.

5. Refer to the instructions for the Double-sided Fusible Web method on page 16 as you work on the following steps.

6. Use the templates you made in step 1 to trace 48 A leaves and 47 A reversed leaves on to the paper side of the fusible web, leaving at least ½in between shapes. In a similar manner, trace four B leaves and three B reversed leaves, 80 flowers and 80 flower centers.

7. Fuse the traced appliqué shapes for the flowers and leaves to an assortment of black and white print fabrics. (Caroline chose to also make a small number of lime green leaves for added interest.) Fuse the flower centers to the lime green fabric. Cut all the shapes out on the traced lines.

MAKE THE CENTER BLOCK

1. Use a ¼in bias maker or your preferred method to turn under the edges of the bias strip cut for the stems in the center block. You will need 34 lengths ranging from 1½in to 3½in. Referring to the photograph, pin or glue lengths of bias in place for the stems so that one end will sit either under another stem or under the heart when it is stitched on top.

2. Referring to the instructions for blind hem stitch, appliqué the vines in place using monofilament thread in the top of the machine.

3. Join the 1in bias strips cut for the center heart together, end to end, to make one long strip. It needs to be at least 60in long. Use a ½in bias maker or your preferred method to turn under the edges of the bias strip. Pin or glue the strip in place over the outline of the heart that you traced. Turn under the first ¼in of the strip, and start at the top inner point of the heart shape. Miter the bottom point and tuck the tail of the bias strip under the folded beginning edge when you return to the top inner point. Make sure that the bias strip covers the ends of the stems.

4. Appliqué the heart in place as you did with the stems, working blind hem stitch using monofilament thread.

5. Remove the backing paper from one of the prepared leaves and position it at the end of a stem. Fuse it in place, then blanket stitch around the edges with black cotton or rayon thread. Refer to the instructions for blanket stitching on page 22. Caroline recommends that you fuse and stitch a few leaves at a time to avoid any fraying of the raw edges.

6. When you have stitched a leaf at the end of all the stems, trim the background square to 38in, with the appliqué centered.

ADD BORDER 1

1. Trim two of the 2in strips of black and white polka dot fabric #1 to 38in. Sew them to the left and right edges of the quilt. Press the seams away from the quilt center.

2. Trim the remaining two strips of black and white polka dot fabric #1 to 41in, and sew them to the top and bottom edges of the quilt. Press as before.

ADD BORDER 2

1. Trim two of the 10½in strips of hot pink hand dyed fabric to 41in. Join three of the remaining three 10½in strips together end to end to make one long strip. From it trim two 61in lengths.

2. Fold each of the four border strips in half, short edges matching, and finger press to crease. Unfold. Then fold the strips in half, long edges matching, and finger press to crease. Unfold.

3. Place the Border 2 Curve Position Guide on one of the border strips, with the straight edge sitting on the center crease and the center mark on the curved edge aligned with the center of the strip (see Diagram 1). Lightly iron the freezer paper in place. Don't use steam, as it will distort the freezer paper. Trace around the curved edge lightly with a pencil, tailor's chalk or the edge of a dry, thin sliver of soap.

4. Lift the freezer paper off the fabric and turn it 180 degrees. Position it back on the fabric with the straight edge on the center crease of the fabric, and the top of the template matching the bottom of the line you just traced (see Diagram 2). Again, trace lightly around the curved edge.

5. Continue working in this manner, placing the curve

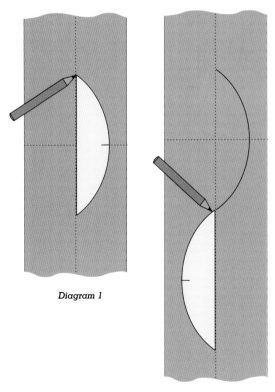

Diagram 1

Diagram 2

of the template alternately to the left and right of the center crease and tracing it to create a continuous curve down the length of each border strip.

6. Use the Border 2 Corner Guide at the ends of each of the longer strips (see Diagram 3).

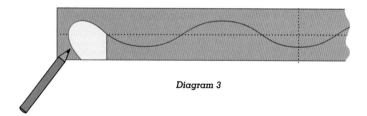

Diagram 3

7. Remove the backing paper from the flower centers and fuse and them to the flowers. Keep the backing paper on the flowers at this stage, as it will act as a stabilizer. Stitch in place using blanket stitch worked in black thread.

8. Remove the backing paper from the flowers and position them over the curved lines that you have drawn. Use 15 flowers on each of the two shorter border strips and 25 flowers on each of the two longer border strips. The easiest way to position them is to place a flower on the 'hill' or 'valley' of each curve, and then place a flower on each side of it.

9. When you are happy with the arrangement, fuse the flowers in place. Then stitch them using blanket stitch, as before.

10. Sew the two shorter border strips to the left and right edges of the quilt. The curve in the center of each strip should be orientated towards the center of the quilt if the corner curves are to align properly.

11. Then sew the two longer strips to the top and bottom edges of the quilt. Press seams away from the center of the quilt.

ADD BORDER 3

1. Sew the 2in strips cut from black and white polka dot fabric #2 end to end , using 45 degree seams, to make one long strip. Press the seams open. From it cut two strips 61in and two strips 64in.

2. Sew the shorter strips to the left and right edges of the quilt. Sew the longer strips to the top and bottom edges of the quilt. Press seams away from the center of the quilt.

ADD BORDER 4

1. Join the remaining seven strips of hot pink hand dyed fabric end to end using straight seams to make one long strip. From it trim two strips 65in and two strips 85in – all these strips are cut a little longer than needed to allow for some 'shrinkage' as they are appliquéd.

2. Follow steps 2 – 4 for Border 2 to trace a curved line on each strip (see Diagram 4). Note that the last

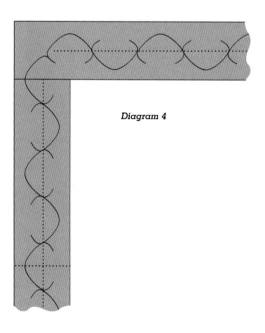

Diagram 4

curve on each end of the strips can't be completed until the borders have been sewn to the quilt.

3. Join the bias strips cut for Border 4 end to end to make one long strip. Use a ¼in bias maker or your preferred method to turn under the edges of the strip. From it, cut 32 lengths each 5¼in long – eight for each border strip. Referring to the photograph, pin or glue the lengths of bias in place so that one end will sit under the long vine when it is placed on top. Stitch them in place as before.

4. Cut the remaining length of bias strip into four equal lengths. Pin or glue a length on each of the border strips, leaving a 12in tail at the beginning and end. Then stitch them in place as before.

5. Remove the backing paper from the leaves and position them at the end of each stem. Fuse them in place, then stitch them using blanket stitch, as before.

6. Trim the two shorter strips to 64in long. Sew them to the left and right edges of the quilt. The curve in the center of each strip should be orientated away from the center of the quilt if the corner curves are to align properly.

7. Trim the two longer strips to 84in long. Sew them to the top and bottom edges of the quilt. Press seams away from the center of the quilt.

8. Iron the corner template in place in one corner, connecting the two bias strips on adjacent borders. Trace around it and then remove it. Glue or pin the tails of bias in place, trimming them as necessary. One strip sits over the end of the first, and a leaf is stitched over the end of the second. Repeat in each corner.

FINISH THE QUILT

1. Press your quilt top ready for quilting and binding. Referring to Preparing the Quilt Top for Quilting in General Quiltmaking Instructions, page 94, layer the backing, batting and quilt ready for quilting. Pin baste.

2. Quilt as desired. *Some Like It Hot* was machine quilted by Caroline. She stitched a double line of 'sketchy' free motion quilting in black thread around the outer edge of the center block. The rest of the top was quilted with monofilament thread, again in a 'sketchy' double line style. As an alternative, you might like to use the leaf and flower shapes as quilting patterns, and fill in around them with swirls.

3. Join the right strips cut for the binding end to end to make one long strip. Use it to bind the quilt, referring to Binding in General Quiltmaking Instructions, page 94.

place on center line of border

Border 2
Curve Position Guide

center

place on center line of border

Border 4
Bias Placement Guide

center

Large Leaf (B)

Small Leaf (A)

Flower

Flower
Center

Love to Machine Appliqué

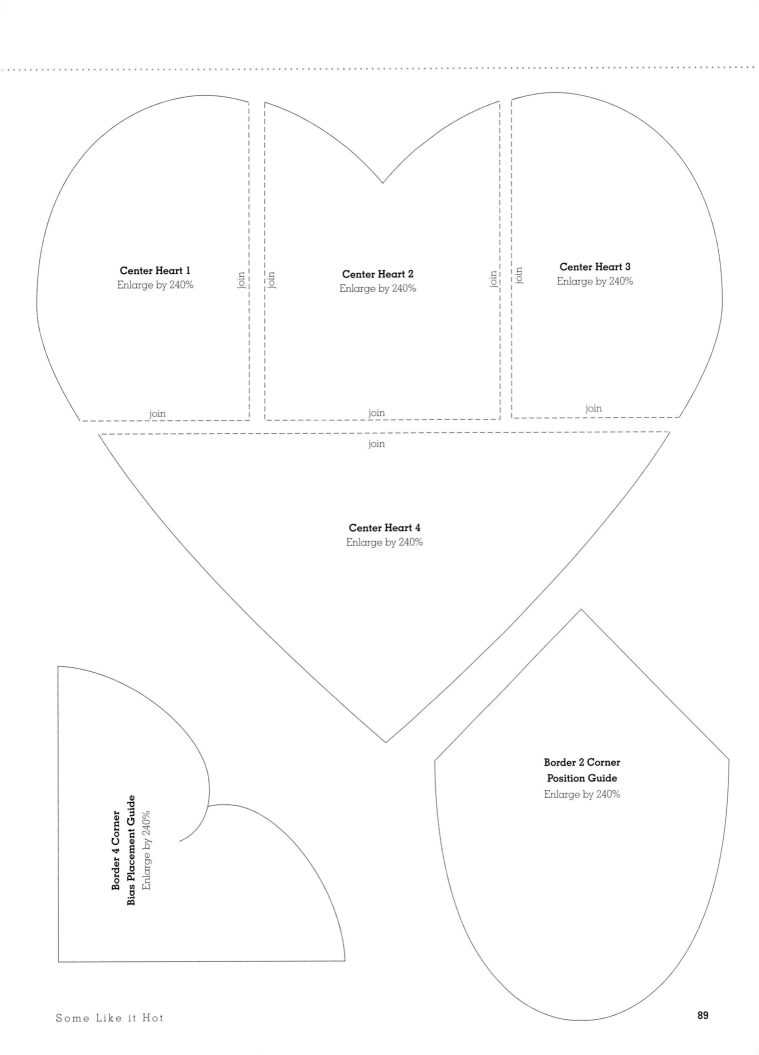

Center Heart 1
Enlarge by 240%

join

join

Center Heart 2
Enlarge by 240%

join

join

Center Heart 3
Enlarge by 240%

join

join

join

Center Heart 4
Enlarge by 240%

**Border 4 Corner
Bias Placement Guide**
Enlarge by 240%

**Border 2 Corner
Position Guide**
Enlarge by 240%

Flower Power

Finished size: 52½in x 33¾in (133cm x 86cm)

Flower Power

Celebrate spring with this delightful wallhanging. Caroline has combined a pastel background made from traditional Rail Fence blocks with bright flowers and butterflies appliquéd with decorative stitching.

MATERIALS:

- ¼yd (20cm) each of 10 pastel hand dyed fabrics (Rail Fence blocks). Caroline used yellow, blue, green, pink and mauve.
- ⅛yd (10cm) each of 10 bright hand dyed fabrics (appliquéd flowers). Caroline used pink, violet, purple and red.
- Scraps of yellow hand dyed fabrics (flower centers)
- ⅜yd (30cm) green hand dyed fabric (stems)
- Butterfly print fabric (broderie perse butterflies). The butterflies on Caroline's quilt range in size from 2in (5cm) to 3in (7.5cm) across.
- ⅜yd (30cm) bright yellow hand dyed fabric (binding)
- 1⅝yd (1.5m) fabric (backing and rod pocket)
- Batting at least 57in x 38in (143cm x 96cm)
- Double-sided fusible web
- 5in (13cm) square of template plastic
- Tear away fabric stabilizer
- Rayon machine embroidery threads to match appliqué fabrics
- Metallic machine embroidery threads in gold, silver, bronze, pink and green
- Monofilament thread (quilting)
- Machine embroidery needles
- Metafil needles
- Compass and pencil
- Rotary cutter, ruler and mat
- Sewing machine
- General sewing supplies

> Method used: Double-sided fusible web; bias tape appliqué
>
> Stitch used: Blanket stitch, satin stitch

CUTTING:

From each of six of the pastel hand dyed fabrics, cut:

- Four strips, 1¾in x width of fabric (Rail Fence blocks)

From each of three of the remaining pastel hand dyed fabrics, cut:

- Five strips, 1¾in x width of fabric (Rail Fence blocks)

From the remaining pastel hand dyed fabric, cut:

- Three strips, 1¾in x width of fabric (Rail Fence blocks)

From the bright yellow hand dyed fabric, cut:

- Five strips, 2¼in x width of fabric (binding)

PIECE THE BACKGROUND

1. Lay out all the strips of pastel hand dyed fabrics in groups of three, mixing the colors. Stitch each group together along their long edges. Press the seam allowance in each strip set in one direction.

2. Crosscut each strip set into 4¼in squares (see Diagram 1). You will need 126 squares in total.

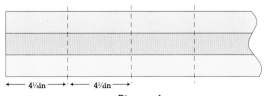

← 4¼in → ← 4¼in →

Diagram 1

3. Lay out the squares in nine rows of 14 squares each, alternating the direction of the blocks. Begin Row 1 with a vertical block, followed by a horizontal block. Make five rows like this. Begin Row 2 with a horizontal block, followed by a vertical block. Make four rows like this.

Row 1 – make 5

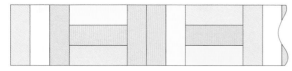

Row 2 – make 4

4. Sew the squares in each row together. Then sew the rows together carefully matching seams. Press.

PREPARE THE APPLIQUÉ

1. Cut a strip of fusible web 8in wide. Lay it diagonally on the wrong side of the green hand dyed fabric, parallel with the bias of the fabric. Fuse it in place.

2. Cut bias strips ⅜in wide across the width of the fusible web (see Diagram 2). The number of strips you require will depend on how you arrange your flowers, and how long each stem is.

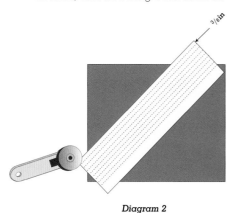

Diagram 2

3. Refer to the instructions for the Double-sided Fusible Web method on page 16 as you work through the following steps.

4. Trace the shapes for the large and small petal on to template plastic and cut them out accurately on the lines. Use these templates to trace 50 of each shape on to the paper side of the fusible web, leaving at least ½in between shapes. Cut the shapes out roughly.

5. Fuse five petal shapes on to the wrong side of each of the bright hand dyed fabrics you have chosen for the flowers. Cut the shapes out accurately on the lines.

6. To make the flower centers, use a compass to draw circles on the paper side of the fusible web. You will need 10 circles with a radius of ⅝in for the large flowers and 10 circles with a radius of ½in for the small flowers. Leave at least ½in between circles.

7. Cut the shapes out roughly. Fuse them to the wrong side of scraps of yellow hand dyed fabrics, then cut them out accurately on the line.

COMPLETE THE APPLIQUÉ

1. Referring to the photo as a guide, arrange the flowers and stems on the Rail Fence background. Five petals are required for each flower: arrange them in a circle, then place a yellow flower center on top, covering the base of each petal by about ¼in. The stems are tucked under one of the petals and curved towards the bottom edge of the quilt.

2. When you are happy with your arrangement, remove the backing paper from the appliqué shapes, one flower and stem at a time, and fuse them in place.

3. Each shape has three rounds of stitching to create a spiky decorative effect. Stitch with metallic green thread on the stems and rayon machine embroidery thread in colors to match the appliqué fabrics for the petals and flower centers. Stitch with the blanket stitching facing away from the appliqué shape – that is, the base (horizontal) stitch should sit on the edge of the appliqué shape and the vertical stitch should overlap onto the background. This may require the

use of a mirror image function on your machine if it has one. For the first round, stitch around the raw edges of each shape. Caroline used a stitch width of 2 and a stitch length of 2.

4. The second round of stitching is blanket stitch with a width of 2 and a stitch length of 3. The third round is blanket stitch with a width of 3 and a stitch length of 3. You will need to move the needle so that the stitches in the third round sit between the stitches formed in the second round.

5. Back your work with tear away stabilizer. Sew around each petal with the same thread using a satin stitch. Caroline set her machine with a stitch width of 2 for the large flowers and 1½ for the small flowers.

6. Using metallic thread, straight stitch three or four lines in the center of each petal to add highlights.

7. Select some butterflies from the print fabric – Caroline used 10 on her quilt. Cut them out at least ¼in outside their edges. Cut pieces of fusible web a little larger than each butterfly and fuse it to the

wrong side of the butterfly fabrics. Then cut out each butterfly on the printed outline.

8. Remove the backing paper and arrange the butterflies on your quilt in a way that pleases you. Fuse in place.

9. Using gold metallic thread, satin stitch the butterflies in place working with a stitch width of 1½in. Stitch the tiny 'feelers' in straight stitch using the same metallic thread.

10. Remove the tear away stabilizer from behind the work.

QUILTING AND BINDING

1. Press your quilt top ready for quilting and binding. Referring to Preparing the Quilt Top for Quilting in General Quiltmaking Instructions, page 94, layer the backing, batting and quilt ready for quilting. Pin baste.

2. Quilt as desired. Because there is more stitching in the lower half of the quilt than the top half, the quilt may have become a little distorted – the lower half may now be a little narrower than the top half. Quilting more densely in the top half will shrink it a little and square the quilt up. Caroline quilted around each shape using monofilament thread. In the top half of the quilt, she used a rayon thread to quilt a large meander.

3. Make a rod pocket if you wish, referring to the General Quiltmaking Instructions, page 94.

4. Join the five strips cut for the binding end to end to make one long strip. Use it to bind the quilt, referring to Binding in General Quiltmaking Instructions, page 94.

Tip: If your sewing machine has a memory, it is possible to combine the second and third rounds of stitching. Set the stitch length at 1½ and the width at 2 and then 3. This will automatically sew the blanket stitch with two different widths to achieve the spiky effect.

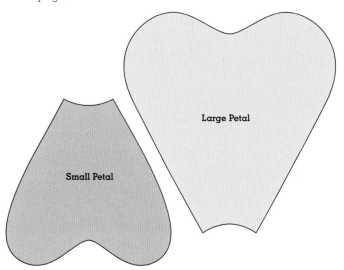

Large Petal

Small Petal

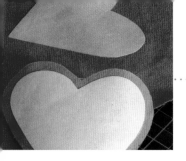

General quiltmaking instructions

Borders:

If strips of fabric need to be joined to make them long enough for the borders of your quilt, it is generally best to sew these joins with a 45 degree seam. These are less noticeable than straight seams but do require more fabric. Fabrics with a striped or checked design will look better with a straight seam

Of course you can always cut fabric parallel to the selvage if you would prefer not to have any joins in your borders. Note, however, that the quantity of fabric listed for the borders for the projects in this book is based on borders being cut across the width of the fabric.

Borders with squared corners:

1. Measure the length of your quilt top in three places – the middle, and near the edge on either side. Add these three measurements together and divide the result by three. This gives the average measurement. Cut the side border strips to this length. This will mean that both side borders will be exactly the same length. If the quilt is not quite square, manipulate it to fit the border strips.

2. With right sides together, pin then stitch the side borders in place. The seam allowance is generally pressed towards the borders.

3. Repeat the above steps for the top and bottom borders, by first measuring the new width of the quilt top and cutting the top and bottom borders to this measurement.

4. When adding the borders to the quilt, find the center of both the border and the edge of the quilt and mark with a pin. Pin the two centers together and then pin both ends of the border to the ends of the quilt. Pin between these points, easing if necessary.

Borders with mitered corners:

Borders with mitered corners can look fantastic, especially when you are using striped or border print fabrics.

1. Measure the quilt top through the center, both

vertically and horizontally. Cut the border strips to this measurement plus twice the cut width of the border plus an extra 2in. This extra 2in allows for seams and is also your 'insurance policy'.

2. Place a pin the center of the borders and also in the center of the edges of the quilt. With right sides together, pin each of borders to the ends of the quilt, in the center and also between these points.

3. Stitch in place, starting and stopping ¼in from the raw edges of the quilt at each end. Backstitch a little. Lightly press the seams towards the borders.

4. Working on one corner at a time, fold the quilt right sides together on the diagonal and bring the unsewn border ends out straight. The border strips are aligned with their outer edges together and straight. The sewn seam lines will lie directly on top of each other.

5. Pin the border strips together using flat-headed flower pins. Use a ruler and pencil to make a 45 degree line that extends across the border from the corner where you stopped stitching. The fold in the quilt will continue along this line.

6. Carefully pin the borders together along the marked line and stitch from the inside corner to the outer edge. Trim the mitered seam to ¼in and press it open.

Preparing the quilt top for quilting

If your quilt top has to be marked for quilting it is best to do this before securing the three layers together.

1. Tape the backing fabric, right side down, to a large flat surface. Caroline uses a table tennis table without the net. The backing fabric should be taut but not stretched.

2. Smooth the batting over the backing fabric. Then smooth the quilt top down on the batting with the right side up.

3. Baste all three layers together. Because all of Caroline's quilts are machine quilted, she uses safety pins to hold the three layers together. On smaller wallhangings you could choose to use quilt basting spray.

4. Pin one edge with pins very close together, then do the same with the opposite edge. The other edges are then done in the same manner.

5. Pin the center of the quilt with pins approximately 4in apart. Whenever possible, Caroline doesn't pin through appliqué shapes that have fusible web underneath them, as it tends to leave a hole that won't close. Pin securely around the edges of the appliqué shape into the background fabric.

6. After quilting has been completed, trim both the batting and the quilt backing to ¼in past the edge of the quilt top. This extra batting and backing fabric will help 'fill out' the binding. This is not always possible of course, as some quilts will need to 'squared up' by cutting through all three layers.

Making a rod pocket

For those quilts that you would like to hang on a wall or exhibit at a quilt show, it is necessary to make a rod pocket or sleeve. Caroline prefers to do this prior to binding the quilt and always tries to use the same fabric that she used for the backing.

1. Measure the width of the trimmed quilt. Cut a 6½in strip of fabric to this length. Turn under a ¼in hem on both ends of the strip. Press. Then turn under another ¼in and stitch.

2. Fold the strip in half lengthwise, wrong sides together and press lightly.

3. Center the rod pocket on the back of the quilt. Align the raw edges with the top of the quilt and pin in place. Baste in place using a long stitch length, removing pins as you go.

The rod pocket is completed after binding is completed.

Binding

Caroline's favourite binding is a continuous, mitered corner binding. Cut the binding strips across the width of the fabric, unless the quilt has curved edges or you are using a striped fabric for the binding. In these cases, cut the binding on the bias. Striped fabric binding cut on the bias looks fantastic as the stripes become diagonal. Caroline usually cuts her binding strips 2¼in wide.

1. To make a continuous, mitered corner binding, join the required number of strips together with 45 degree

seams and trim the seam allowance back to ¼in. Iron the seams open to help distribute the bulk, then press the continuous strip in half lengthwise with wrong sides together.

2. Line up the binding with the edge of the quilt top, raw edges together and about two thirds of the way down one side of the quilt. Leave approximately 6in of binding loose so that it can be joined to the end of the binding.

3. Stitch in place using a ¼in seam allowance and an even-feed walking foot. As long as the binding or quilt is not stretched as you sew, it is not necessary to pin the binding in place. Stop stitching ¼in from the corner of the quilt, leaving the needle in the down position. Pivot, turning the quilt as if to sew down the next edge, but reverse-stitch off the edge instead. Cut the threads and fold the binding straight up to form a 45 degree angle. Finger-press or pin to hold the binding in place. Fold the binding down again with the fold even with the edge of the quilt top. Remove the pin and stitch through all thicknesses, starting on the batting. Continue around all the corners in the same manner until you are approximately 6in from the starting point, leaving the end of the binding unsewn.

4. Remove the quilt from the machine. Cut one end of the binding at a 45 degree angle , and turn it under ¼in. Tuck the other end inside this one (trimming if necessary) and carefully pin and slip stitch in place.

5. The binding is now ready to be rolled to the back of the quilt and hand stitched firmly in place. The front miters will fold in one direction and the back of the miters will fall in the other direction. This helps to distribute the bulk on the corners. The top edge of the binding will also cover the raw edges of the rod pocket, which was basted in place earlier.

Finishing the rod pocket

Fold the fabric of the rod pocket to the top of the quilt, nearly to the finished edge of the binding.

Pin the bottom of the rod pocket in place and hand stitch securely, creating a slight bulge of fabric on the top of the rod pocket. The hanging rod will sit in this bulge of the rod pocket and when hung, the quilt will sit flat against the wall.

Caroline Price

Caroline lives at Pyramul, near Mudgee, in New South Wales, Australia. The area is well known for its superfine wool and its superb wines. Caroline and husband John have five adult children who have all left home to make their own way in the world. Their greatest gift to both Caroline and John are their beloved grandchildren.

Caroline has been quilting 'seriously' for approximately 15 years. After selling her fabric shop, Caroline was diagnosed with breast cancer and as with many others, quilting definitely became a form of therapy.

Many of her quilts have been published in Australian quilting magazines. This is her third book. The first was *A Quilter's Garden – Machine Appliqué* and the second was *Rapt in Borders*, which was co-authored by close friend, Michelle Marvig.

Caroline teaches regularly. She has conducted workshops not only all over Australia, but also in New Zealand. She has also demonstrated and lectured at Quilt Market in Houston, USA. Whilst machine appliqué is her first love, she also teaches students to make quilts that are predominately pieced. Encouraging students to learn new techniques that can be used to make their own designs is a joy and many friends have been made along the way.

Caroline can be contacted on price@activ8.net.au

Acknowledgments:

Many people helped me along the way with this book and I wish to thank:
- My husband, John for his unerring support and brilliant eye for detail and colour.
- Larraine Smith for her beautiful longarm quilting on the pastel version of *Love Affair – Heart Sampler, Hidden Treasures* and *Clementine Vines*.
- Gail Simpson of Cotton Patch Fabrics, who dyed all the hand dyed fabrics used in the quilts.
- Michelle Marvig for her friendship and all the long distance phone calls to discuss the quilts.
- My publishers and editors, Karen Fail and Megan Fisher and The American Quilter's Society for their trust and support both of me and other Australian quilters.
- Bernina Australia for their wonderful machine and support.